SIGNS OF AGNI YOGA

FIERY WORLD

II

FIERY WORLD

II

1934

Agni Yoga Society
319 West 107th Street
New York NY 10025
www.agniyoga.org

People usually have absolutely no idea how to use the given Teaching. When they hear some formula which seems familiar, they haughtily exclaim, "Again the same thing, known to everyone!" They do not attempt to verify the extent to which this familiar formula has been realized and applied by them. They do not stop to think that the useful Teaching is given not for the sake of novelty but for the upbuilding of a worthy life.

The Teaching of Life is not a compilation of unheard-of utopias. Humanity is of very ancient origin; and in the course of ages multifarious sparks of Wisdom have been poured upon Earth, but every cycle has its key. If someone can recognize the present key as a familiar one, then let him rejoice and be thankful for an indication which is close to him. It seems simple, but in reality it proves to be very difficult. People love to listen to news and to receive toys, but few are ready to refine their consciousness.

It cannot be that one of the elements has not been stressed in the Teachings. Fire has been mentioned a thousand times, but now the stressing of Fire is no longer a repetition, for it is a warning about events which concern the planet's fate. Most people will not be able to say that in their hearts they have been preparing for the Fiery Baptism, although the most ancient Teachings forewarned about the inevitable Epoch of Fire.

FIERY WORLD

Part II

1. Now let us approach still closer to the study of the conditions of the Fiery World. The divisibility of the spirit may call forth many questions. One may certainly ponder to what an extent the chemism of the Luminaries influences the separated portions of the spirit. During long distance flights parts of the spirit may be exposed to the most varied influences. Indeed, even the fiery bodies cannot avoid various influences, but an open consciousness will always help to find the better vibrations. From the earthly state of consciousness it is difficult to control the separated parts of the spirit, and these messengers of the spirit mostly adapt themselves to the local conditions. Therefore, they may sometimes be very clear and audible and sometimes very hazy, in all manifestations. Such a condition is created not by the spirit of the sender and not even by the one who receives, but by the chemism of the currents. Even the most Fiery Beings are subject to cosmic currents. This by no means diminishes their lofty nature, but only confirms the immutable laws. One must be imbued with the majesty of the Universe to such an extent that one accepts the laws of the Great Luminaries.

When we look in wonderment at the Chinese carved ivory spheres, one can imagine how great must be the tension of will for the condensation of mass in the formation of heavenly bodies.

2. To come to the realization of the necessity not to diminish the attainment of the acceptance of the law,

will be already the joy of the spirit. To understand how the Great Planetary Spirits revere discipline, will be already the joy of the spirit. To realize the fiery being within oneself, will be already the joy of the spirit. But to understand this being as a very great responsibility, will be valor.

I affirm that there is no greater joy for Us than to see you accept these qualities of the spirit. The fiery consciousness is already the finest chemism. It manifests most fully in the interplanetary spaces. Where the physical body feels already exhausted, there begins the fiery breath. Therefore, beings are divided into two types—one thrives in the depths of the lower strata, and the other aspires towards summits.

3. Fiery healing by far-off currents is obvious, but people will try to deny it. The coarsest form of electricity will be accepted, but the currents of highest tension will be actually ridiculed. Yet useful people more than once have been able to feel these salutary vibrations. The rhythms indicated long ago certainly do not exhaust many other vibrations, from strongly affecting tremors to the most subtle.

I wish now to point out a very important circumstance. Even under the impact of these cosmic currents the human will has a great significance. He who does not wish to accept these currents will experience a very moderate reaction, but voluntary acceptance will give a very accelerated effect. Of course, there also may be a third circumstance—when the link with Hierarchy is firm and conscious, then, both for the Sender and for the receiving one, the manifestation of best obtainable effects is easy. Not without reason did I direct your attention to this mutually facilitating energy. It will help to conserve energy, and this is of great importance, especially now when there are so many cross-currents.

One may easily remember occasions when during the action of useful currents the receiving one persistently repeated—"my bed is strongly shaken, of course it is from an earthquake." By such lightminded denials people often diminish the influence of most effective energies.

Let the fiery healing compel people to ponder about Those Who apply Their best efforts for the benefit of humanity.

4. There are no shadows in the Fiery World. This is not difficult to imagine, because even upon earth it is possible if one arranges the sources of light properly. The luminosity of all parts of the Fiery World produces a continuous glow. Thus also is consciousness permanently awake, for there is no sleep. Such tension becomes possible when the inner fire completely corresponds to the cosmic one, but in full harmony the tension is not felt.

It is quite just to call the music of the spheres the Song of Fire. Are not the fiery vibrations concordant? And is not this resounding nurtured with radiations? Thus when we call Agni "the Keeper of the Gates" and understand the unutterable link, then we too resound. One may resound also here, if only for a moment, then all earthly habits become obsolete. Thus one must affirm in the heart all sparks of the Fiery World. May the earthly habits be replaced by the Fiery Truth.

5. Let us remember the myth about the "Origin of Mountains." When the Planetary Creator toiled over the formation of the earth, He gave attention to fertile plains which could provide people with a quiet agriculture. But the Mother of the World said, "Verily, people will find bread and trade in the plains, but when gold will pollute the plains whither shall go the pure in spirit to gather strength? Either let them have wings, or let them have mountains, in order to escape from gold." And the Creator answered, "It is too early to give wings to people, they would carry death and destruction. But let us give them mountains. Even if some be afraid of them, for others they will be salvation." Thus there are two kinds of people—people of the plains and people of the mountains.

One may remember now these myths, which foretold the contamination of the planet. Indeed, why do people investigate so little the chemism of the air? Even with earthly apparatus one may record the condensation of destructive substances. Of course not always can these currents be detected, just as is the case with the photographing of the manifestations of the Subtle World, which will not always be successful, but with patience much can be recorded. The Fiery World does not easily lend itself to earthly observations.

6. Let us recall the myth about the "Origin of Lightning." The Mother of the World said to the Creator, "When the Earth will be covered with dark veils of malice, how will the salutary drops of Bliss penetrate?" And the Creator answered, "Torrents of Fire may be gathered which can pierce the thickest layer of darkness." The Mother of the World said, "Verily, the sparks of Fire of Thy Spirit can give salvation, but who will collect and guard them for use when needed?" The Creator replied, "Trees and herbs will preserve My sparks, but when the leaves fall off, then let the deodar and its sisters preserve throughout the year their accumulations of Fire." Thus in various myths there has been reflected the link with the Higher World. Everywhere there has been stressed solicitude about humanity and all creatures. Likewise did the ancient priests carefully watch over the correct distribution of the creative Fire.

Nowadays man crosses fruits and plants without proper supervision, but one should observe through lengthy experiments how best to preserve the fiery substance. One must not lightmindedly interfere with the creativeness of Nature. The best counsels can be given from the Fiery World, but one should seek this Benefaction.

7. Now you are not astonished that the Battle lasts so long, because the expansion of consciousness extends the boundaries of the being. Indeed it would be lightmindedness to think that the One Who revolted against Light were a weakling. One must understand that the Forces of Light refrain from annihilating the enemy not because of weakness, but because of a desire not to upset prematurely the equilibrium of the planet. Few are able to realize that the power of the Creator of the planet takes into consideration physical conditions. But one may already see that the harmonious vibrations have been disturbed and that the planet is being shaken in convulsions of heat and cold. Therefore I advise the equilibrium of the spirit. There where the foundation is affected, there a special presence of the spirit is necessary.

Even in popular books you read about the changes of climate, about the changes of continents and currents. Let there seem much inaccuracy, but the science of Luminaries is exact. Let it not be thought that the prophecies are erroneous, for they come from the Fiery World.

8. Agni Yoga requires a special resourcefulness. It cannot manifest through physical mechanics, which appear in different degrees in other Yogas. Such an element as Fire should, it would seem, be subject to

physical laws no less than other elements. But the essence of Agni is subject to such very subtle laws, that physically it is inexpressible. Thus one must apply the entire refined resourcefulness in order to follow the fiery signs. Hence, one may perceive that often fiery signs are sent by Hierarchy, and people do not even try to perceive them and to apply them. The fiery laws lie at the very foundation of human life. Conception, birth and all acts subject to Agni do not arouse wonderment at the manifestation of the Ineffable. One may wander around the mechanical constructions, but advance into the future is possible only through realization of Agni. When whole continents are dying, how are new abodes to be found without new energy? It is necessary to prepare the spiritual consciousness for great earthly upheavals—this at best, but if people approach the last divide filled with the black hatred of the past, they will be but powder magazines. Thus let us resourcefully think about Agni.

9. It is not superfluous to point out to people that they have been neglectful in not thinking most steadfastly about the future. The myth about Gold has been mentioned already; it spoke about the time when the thought about Gold will become more persistent and will indicate the approach of the time of Fire, the manifest antipode of Gold. People often have read about the fiery destruction of the planet. Two thousand years ago it was pointed out that Fire would devour the Earth. Many thousands of years ago the Patriarchs warned humanity of the fiery peril. Science has failed to pay attention to many signs. No one is willing to think on a planetary scale. Thus We speak before the awesome time. One may still not escape the last hour. Help can be extended, but hatred will not be a healer.

10. Pay attention to the so-called transitory states

of the organism. The state between sleep and wakefulness provides a very significant field for observations. One may notice how amidst earthly thinking fragments of thought of a different order intrude, objects seem to vibrate and the earthly perception is altered. Few admit the thought that this different kind of perception is the thinking of the Subtle, and even Fiery World. As the manifested world disappears, one awakens to the voice of the Subtle World. Amidst various transitory states one can notice the lightnings of the Higher Worlds. Thus, one should attentively observe the special resoundings. Amidst earthly conditions one should not merge into these manifestations, because equilibrium is of first importance, but the receptacle of an expanded consciousness must find a place for manifestations of all three worlds. Only thus shall we become accustomed to the understanding of the fiery thought. Fire, as a visible element, often impedes the realization of the fiery thought, but the manifestation of Agni is not a match. Yet every fiery manifestation first of all reflects upon the thinking process. Meanwhile pay attention to the origination of the visible Fire—the bright energy whirls in spirals, so that even in a small flame one may see the process of intervention of an outside energy. The moment of blending of the inner Fire with the outer one can be called resonant in beauty.

11. Some blind people can sense the presence of fire by sound instead of light. Some even prefer to cognize by sound rather than by heat. One may conduct instructive experiments not only upon blind people but also upon heavily blindfolded people. But of course the blindfold may interfere with the general sensitiveness, therefore the testimonies of blind people will be more convincing. The more so since their

hearing is usually more acute. They may even testify that the flame of the candle resounds. We have refined our senses in many respects, but the physical deprivation of one sense sharpens the other. The sighted people perceive the song of the fire in a stove, in a bonfire, and in a conflagration, in other words in the crudest manifestation. And besides, people but seldom distinguish the sounding of the fire from the noise of the burning material. Nevertheless it is possible to know the resounding of fire.

The Chinese of antiquity tried to reproduce the fiery sounding on string instruments. The Emperor of Fire in his temple had to be accompanied by a fiery sounding. Likewise, the Ruler of the Waters had to be accompanied by crystal instruments. Of course such refinement is now forgotten, but it indicated a great keenness of observation of the soundings of Nature. It is useful even to remember about such cults based upon the finest vibrations. Verily, not cold reasoning, but the tremor of the heart will bring closer the fiery refinement. Besides, not fire-worship but the veneration of Agni, as the beginning of the link with the Higher World, should be laid into the foundation.

12. You understand Our tension, when the manifestation of the brain is like a raging fire. But Our enemies rely upon the limits of physical possibilities. The more so must one oppose them with whole patience. Truly it is difficult to find saints who were not afflicted with special ailments. Many times even they failed to understand why they should suffer such pains, but the fiery tension cannot be avoided when pursuing the shortest path. Could it be otherwise when the feet are upon Earth and the head in the Fiery World!

13. One should observe not only Ours but also the Black Brotherhood. It is erroneous to minimize the

strength of the dark forces. Very often their victory is due to such neglect. People very often say, "They are not worth thinking about." But one ought to think about everything existing. If people justifiably protect themselves against thieves and murderers, so much the more should they guard against the assassins of the spirit. One should appraise their strength in order better to withstand them. Ur. fearlessly visited the dark ones. She saw many of different grades, and in her valor she addressed them. Verily, there exists such a degree of courage that even the power of darkness is silenced. True, it is impossible to ever convince the dark ones, but one may paralyze them and considerably weaken them. Therefore, it is so important to oppose darkness actively. Out of dead dust—only dust is born. For the sake of home cleanliness various brooms are used. And when one finds a scorpion in the house, then it is immediately removed.

Ur. has seen a disciplined meeting of the dark ones, and many convening humans could learn much from such a meeting. Ur. spoke justly, as Our Messenger, and in such an affirmation there lies great power. One must not restrain the force, when the spirit knows wherein lies the weapon. The dark ones discuss especially intensively when they see that the events are not shaping themselves in favor of their ruler. The Forces of Light prevent them from destroying you. It would seem to be not difficult to annihilate peaceful people, but above all the dark resources there exists the power of the spirit. Ur. rightly said to them, "You consider Satan invincible, but I testify to his defeat before all of you." Thus, one may know about the intentions of the dark ones and about Our Power.

But those who think that visions and dreams are caused by indigestion, can easily sleep through the most valuable signs of reality. Only those who know the strength of their adversaries can hope for victory. What discipline and unity one must manifest to overcome such powerful gatherings! One must gather all spiritual courage to remove and put an end to petty things.

14. At a time when one sacrifices his soul for the good of the World, the other sits upon the water. While one offers his heart for the salvation of his fellow-men, the other flounders in the manifestations of the Subtle World. The saints of Great Service have no psychism, because they are always striving in spirit towards Hierarchy, and their heart resounds to the anguish of the World. Psychism is a window into the Subtle World, but the teacher tells the pupil, "Do not turn so often to the window, look into the book of life."

Often psychism proves to be a weakening influence, but the Great Service is in straight-knowledge. Therefore We warn against psychism, against turning one's gaze backwards without a definite object for the future. The spiritually weak psychists are often a tasty dish for the satanists.

Verily, in the Great Service is the feeling of great responsibility. But one should become accustomed to this chalice, for there can be no shortest path without emptying it. The heart which aspires to Hierarchy feels how necessary and salutary is the Chalice of Offering. To some it is only object of derision and condemnation, but to others it is a precious treasure. It is Our great desire that the true straight-knowledge be developed.

15. Nothing can so much turn one away from the path as the rejection of straight-knowledge. But the beginning of straight-knowledge lies in the devotion to Hierarchy. Only true devotion will prevent one from polluting the straight-knowledge by personal egoism. Only devotion will teach not to distort the Indications of the Teacher. Only devotion will help to find new strength. I will not weary of repeating about true devotion, because often people substitute for this concept the most abominable fanaticism. Thus the Fiery World is ordained.

16. As in Heaven, so on Earth. One foundation of Be-ness verily permeates all existence. Precisely this foundation should help humanity to understand the Hierarchy of Infinity. Who then will doubt that in every earthly object is expressed someone's will?

Without will no earthly object can be created, nor set into motion. Thus it is upon Earth, and it is the same in the Higher World. Since the existence of the planet as an earthly stronghold requires an impulse of will, it is just as comprehensible that whole systems of heavenly bodies require the same. Such will of course is more readily comprehensible to an expanded consciousness. But even the average human will can serve as an example of a microcosm. One need not go too far in special calculation, but if we take as a unit the human will at its highest tension, then it is possible to estimate the force of the impulse of the planetary will. One may be involved in innumerable ciphers, in calculating the will-impulse of a whole system. Such a problem would be an introduction into the Grandeur of the Ineffable. So useful are the observations, therefore, upon will power, when thought sets into motion this cosmic energy. The abode of Agni is the furnace of Cosmic Power. One should not be overwhelmed at the innumerable digits in the calculation of the Magnitude. Figures merely express that of which we are conscious, but the fiery heart, without figures, can strive along the path of assimilation of the Grandeur there where word is naught.

17. Rhythm is the progenitor of cooperation. From hoary antiquity people have understood the significance of rhythmic choirs, of musical movements; thus has the consciousness accumulated knowledge about the impelling force of collective labor. People knew long ago that rhythm kindled collective fires and helped in avoiding irritation and disunity. It affirmed identical aspirations, therefore music is the sign of unity before collective work. It is a pity that modern music is so often lacking in rhythm. Perhaps it serves as the beginning of many spiritual ulcers, but the question of harmony is unusually complicated. Lack of rhythm is disunity, but crude rhythm is stupor. Thus only a fiery consciousness will prompt the refinement of rhythm. One may ponder over many things, but we shall always return to the fiery understanding. The abode of Agni is opened not by reasoning but by the harmony of rhythm. Precisely as a vessel sometimes is opened not by force but by rhythm. Only the true rhythm carries us forward and preserves us from delay. Yet we know all the detrimental result of delay, as in movement, so also in the spirit. It is inadmissible to have a broken rhythm, at times retarded and at other times accelerated. Thus an enormous and useless expenditure of energy takes place. He will not retreat who has begun to advance in fiery rhythm. Precisely this rhythm saves one from sorrowful ponderings and leads one forward in spirit; therefore let us not limit the effectiveness of the rhythm by external motion only, let us introduce it into spiritual life.

18. People feel sometimes something singing within them. Such a song is never disharmonious. One can rejoice when such vibrations stir one's being. In them is contained the embryo of attainment.

19. The great heat is not only from physical causes but from a chemical condensation which has gathered over the planet—the forerunner of the Fiery Epoch. People pay no attention to such signs, but it is primarily people themselves who can improve the situation. Malice is a condenser of heavy chemism. People do not want to believe that their inner laboratory has a cosmic significance. People ponder over various useless things, but they do not wish to reflect about their own importance and responsibility. Of course the chemical heat is as yet only temporary, and will be replaced by cold. One may imagine what people are preparing for themselves a quarter of a century hence! There is still time to think and to render the atmosphere wholesome.

20. There are many reasons why people fear the Subtle World and radiations of light. They feel in their essence that in the Subtle World every intention is accompanied by an obvious radiation, but man himself does not see his own radiations. If he were fully convinced of the good quality of his thoughts, he would fear nothing. But with a majority of people thoughts are very sinuous, and man, through the earthly habit of doubt, errs much from the true foundations of thinking. Therefore I reiterate so much about the necessity of clear thinking. One should be so sure of the quality of one's own thinking that not for an instant could one be confused by one's own light. A firm aspiration towards good, affirmed by the heart, will only multiply the beautiful lights. Besides their essence these lights are as purifiers of space. In the Subtle World such benevolent radiations create an all-embracing smile and contribute towards general joy. Therefore affirm yourself in good, and think so as not to be ashamed before any one. Do not consider these words an abstraction. The Subtle World confirms them. Many dwellers in the Subtle World regret that no one on Earth told them about these obvious radiations, which ought to be beautiful.

21. Many would like to ask to be taught how to enter the Subtle World, but they do not know how to ask without appearing ridiculous. But let the Writings circulate throughout the world, let them be read, if even secretly. Let them be derided during the day and read by night. One may forgive these errors, for no one has given these people a simple guiding formula. Some frightened them, some lulled their consciousness, some lead them away from Truth, but no one indicated to them the beautiful transition to the Summits of Existence. Let us not reproach, but just lately there has been especially much confusion in the world. True, the fact of the existence of the Subtle World is somewhat strengthened in the consciousness, but still people do not know how to deal with such facts and how to reconcile them with the routine of life. They are attempting to pass in silence that which loudly proclaims itself.

Thus in the morning hour as well as in the evening let us get accustomed to the thought of the crossing into the Beautiful World. Let it be Beautiful for us.

22. Raj-Agni—thus was called that Fire which you call enthusiasm. Truly this is a beautiful and powerful Fire, which purifies all surrounding space. The constructive thought is nurtured upon this Fire. The thought of magnanimity grows in the silvery light of the Fire of Raj-Agni. Help to the near ones flows from the same source. There is no boundary line, no limitations for the wings radiant with Raj-Agni. Do not think that this Fire can be kindled in an evil heart. One must develop in oneself the ability to call forth the source of such transport. At first one must prepare in oneself the assurance that the heart is offered to the Great Service. Then one should reflect that the glory of the works is not one's own, but belongs to the Hierarchy of Light. Then it is possible to become uplifted by the infinitude of Hierarchy and affirm oneself in the heroic attainment needed for all worlds. Thus not for oneself, but in the Great Service is kindled Raj-Agni. Understand that the Fiery World cannot stand without this Fire.

23. Many experiments take place during the flights to high altitudes. Perhaps the investigators understand in the depth of their being that at great altitudes they can find much needed information. But besides physical instruments they must provide themselves with psychic energy; only then will such experiments really give a new conception. It is necessary that the investigators of heights and depths have a psychic training. Only through such a combination will the physical side of the work also acquire a special significance.

24. You do well in leaving people to decide for themselves. One may point out a useful direction, but every coercion is already against the law. Above all one should not forcibly kindle the Fires. The Fiery World can be attained only through one's own heart. No one was ever forcibly led into the Fiery Realm. People often do not understand wherein lies the boundary of violence. Some tend to use violence, others seek violence—both are against the nature of the Fire.

25. Note the densification of the atmosphere. Unusual are these low dense layers. Truly the crust of the planet is dying, deprived of Benevolent Influences. One must hurry with a new condition of purification.

26. One may observe different types of people, who can be distinguished according to their natures. Some do not think about the future, fulfilling, as it were, their entire purpose in this earthly life. Others strive forward with their whole spirit, for them earthly life does not present any finality. Even if not highly refined, these people sense with the heart that everything is ahead of them. Have dealings with the latter, for notwithstanding their errors they will be still striving into the future, and thus will already belong to the Truth. You know that Agni lives in the hearts of those who love the future. Even if their Agni is not yet manifested, its potentiality is inexhaustible. Likewise look with compassion upon people who do not know the future, as upon the sick. And truly their aura will not be luminous, for it will be deprived of the radiation of Materia Lucida. Many people have formed such privation for themselves, that they cannot even manifest through the opaque substance of the nerves. As imperil obstructs the movement of the fiery substance, so a limited thinking makes the precious substance turbid. One may heal these diseases through hypnotic suggestion.

27. One may influence plants, as has been shown, but one must exercise great patience, because every atmospheric current can affect the transmission of the fiery energy. But who can imagine that the cosmic chemism does not influence the human organism! But it is correctly observed that even the fragrance of flowers can change under the pressure of cosmic currents. Be not astonished that all Nature responds to that which man does not wish to notice. The refinement of consciousness primarily depends on attention to the surroundings.

28. Salamanders, as entities of the lower fire, cannot

be very luminous. When I showed you a salamander I wished to give you a conception of the creatures of the fiery depths. I have already shown you the subterranean and submarine entities, but one must also know the amplitude of Fire. One can understand better the entire diversity of the Fiery entities when not only the Highest but also the lowest is perceived.

29. Verily one may operate upon the spleen. Physically the organism can exist for some time even without it, but this will be a purely physical solution. Up to the present people have not cared about the consequences for the subtle body. Whereas, the organ which is connected with the subtle body must be greatly protected but not destroyed. The same takes place in the removal of the appendix; man not only lives but even gains weight, yet one of the main functions of the psychic energy is disorganized. The appendix absorbs the psychic elements of food. Someone may live even without such elements, but why deprive the organism of such helpers? Of course all physical operations upon the heart show how far physicians are from the psychic problem. Therefore it is very needful to avoid all physical operations, if the conditions needed for the subtle body are not observed. Unavoidable operations should be accompanied by corresponding suggestion, in order that the parts of the subtle body may assume the required position. One should mentally contact the subtle body. If the thought affirms through suggestion the fiery self-protection then a multitude of ill consequences will be avoided. Such self-protection is especially necessary against all infections. If during an operation one could suggest the necessary processes, the help of the subtle body would considerably contribute to the desired result. Such suggestions can regulate all the functions of the organism, but without this assistance it is sad to see how the subtle bodies are mutilated.

A surgeon in ancient China before an operation usually made his patient's subtle body leave the physical one, and then by suggestion he explained to it the new adaptation of the organ. Thus, not only physical conditions should be taken into consideration.

30. Some people may think—how easy it is for the Lords, when They have passed beyond the boundaries of earthly burdens! But whoever says this does not know the scope of reality. Precisely as it is upon Earth, so also in Heaven. The earthly burdens pass away, but incomparable cosmic cares take their place. Truly, if it is difficult on Earth, then so much more difficult it is in Heaven. Let us not count the moments of Devachan, when illusion may conceal tomorrow's labor. But in action amidst chaos, it cannot be easy. You suffer from darkness and chaos. In all abodes it is as difficult from many aspects of darkness and the same chaos. But, fortunately for you, you only feel the attacks of chaos and do not see its murky movements. Truly, it is difficult for people because of their ignorance and their servility to darkness. But it is more difficult when one sees the movements of the masses of matter being turned into chaos. When the destructive subterranean fire tries prematurely to pierce the earthly crust, or when layers of gases poison the space, the difficulty surpasses all earthly imagination. Not burdens, but only comparisons help now to speak about the difficulties. For ignoramuses think that hymns and harps are the lot of Heavenly Dwellers. Such error must be dispersed. Nowhere are there indications that it is difficult only upon Earth; in comparison it must be said—if here one is annoyed by devils, the Archangel is threatened by Satan himself. Thus one must understand action and the everlasting battle with chaos. One must realize it as the only path and grow to love it as the sign of the Creator's trust.

31. One must become accustomed to the fact that every message from Us is something indispensable. Be this one word or one letter of the alphabet, yet if it is sent, it means it is needed. People themselves often pronounce a command in one word, but often they associate it with something lasting. Thus also from the Watch Tower it is often possible to send only one letter.

32. The whirlwind is not generated, where it already roars. Lightning is perceived by Us when it is being generated in tension. Thus We feel the formation of whirlwinds. Let them pass unnoticed by those who should not notice them. Let the course of destiny be as an underground stream, yet all neighboring examples do not pass without consequences. Let the pre-ordained take place.

33. One must learn how to encourage spiritual people. True, they achieve heroic deeds not for the sake of encouragement, but still they are in need of safeguarding of their spiritual direction. Every ruler must know not only the power of censure, but must also understand the good of encouragement. The latter is more difficult, but what a benefaction is derived when the ruler knows what each one needs for the blooming of his "lotus." There may be many anchorites, but their beneficial tension will not produce the highest measure of energy if the surrounding forces are hostile. Therefore the heart must be strengthened in the striving to understand the very best.

34. A mother sometimes spoke to her son about the meaning of Highest Bliss, and of the eternal link with the Higher Forces. One day the boy very attentively observed a little bird on the window-sill, and

whispered to his mother—"It also watches me so that I should not say something bad!" Thus may one begin the thought about the great link.

35. There is no reason for a scholar to think that the substance of the emanation of the fingertips is only poisonous. It depends entirely upon the spiritual state. The imperil of a nervous observer, of course will give poisonous sediments if he pays no attention to the spiritual condition of his organism. The ability to discern differences in nervous conditions will give to the scientists an incomparable possibility. For even the phosphorescence of the fingertips varies. And every radiation is based upon chemism.

36. After a new cataclysm humanity will enter upon the path of cooperation. But one may imagine what two hostile neighbors must outlive in order to think about mutual benefit. The oppression of one has been the rejoicing of the other. It means that they both must suffer. The devices of the dark forces will help the especially cunning ones to protect themselves. The manifestation of justice is very difficult, if the motives are not taken into consideration.

37. The manifestation at night had two meanings. Firstly, it has shown to what an extent thoughts are fulfilled in the Subtle World if consciousness is expanded. Thus the thought about an increase in height immediately caused the growth of the subtle body. But this is not beneficial for the physical body; therefore a strong reaction was necessary in order to adjust the subtle body. Such action is rare, and such manifestation of the subtle body is also rare, therefore it should be recorded. It demonstrates how thoughts are realized in the Subtle World. The thought creativeness of the Subtle World is difficult to realize in the earthly state, but a certain degree of development permits perception and even transmittance into the physical brain of the subtle consciousness. During such resetting certain centers must be touched, as it were, and such massage coordinates again the two bodies.

One may eventually observe many significant manifestations. Naturally, at the return of the subtle body a certain exhaling takes place. According to its degree it demonstrates the speed of return of the subtle body. A strong exhalation indicates that the flight has been a hurried one, but such speed usually carries fatigue with it.

You also correctly observed the consequences of improvement in currents. But even such observations are accessible only to the refined consciousness. One may contrive not a few explanations to avoid noting the higher current, but the developed consciousness in such a case will send its gratitude into space. Truly great is the effect of every expression of gratitude! People must accept this law as a living link with the Higher Worlds.

38. Every message must be not only benevolent but also attractive. One may notice that many young people do not follow in the footsteps of their fathers and mothers. Aside from karmic reasons one can notice the unattractiveness of the actions of the elders. The same may be seen in regard to religions. Religion, as the link with the Higher World, must first of all be attractive. Fear is not attractive, violence is repellent, but the very understanding of the Higher World must be attractive. One may rejoice at everything of the Highest. Even the weakminded will not turn away from the Highest. In order to obscure the Highest one must commit a series of repulsive actions. No matter who these repellers may be, they are in any case blasphemers. If they besmirch the most Beautiful, they are servitors of darkness. The answer does not lie in dogmas nor in symbols—one may debase the most beautiful sign. How then to call those who seduce the little ones away from the Abode of God? Seducers and jailers are they who discredit the prayer to the Highest. Has it ever been said that one may speak with one's father and mother only in their own words? So also in the prayer to the Most High—who can force his heart to laud in alien terms? He who composes prayers, hymns, songs, sings with his own heart. The spirit cannot be prevented from soaring upon its own wings. Whither and how will fly the wingless? And will not he who breaks even the smallest feather be responsible? If a song is needed it is the song of the heart, and in this song all creation will resound. Every object will join in lauding the Most High. He who helps his neighbor to create a still more attractive praise will be a creator of good. No dogma can forbid conversing with the Highest. The more beautifully it is done, the nearer will be the approach. But if help is needed, it suffices to express oneself with—"Help." But even for such a simple word attractiveness is needed.

The bigots, of whom you have heard so much, precisely are devoid of such attractiveness. How much darkness and repulsion they have sown! Can there be a language in which one cannot pray? The prayer of spirit is expressed in all languages, likewise can the heart sing in its own language, only if there is resounding of attractiveness.

39. Of course you hear people complain about the uselessness of prayer. They say, "Why hermits and monasteries, when the world sinks in misfortunes?" But no one wants to think what the world would turn into without prayer. Therefore all blasphemy against the deeds of the spirit should cease. Whence will come the feeling of the bond with the Highest, if not from prayer? Let the condemning ones remember—have their hearts not trembled during expressions of rapture? The expressions of the spirit brought nearer the possibility of attainment. Verily one should guard the bridge to the Highest World.

40. Besides the borrowing of energy, the signs of absence and dizziness pertain to the fiery reactions. Likewise are epidemics of neuralgia and of seeming rheumatism nothing else but actions of the fiery centers under the pressure of the spatial Fire. Not soon will people consent to investigate such epidemics under the sign of Fire. People usually like to dissect, but synthesis is difficult for them. Yet it is already time to pay attention to every disease which yields to suggestion. One must clearly visualize the cause which creates physical pains, but which disappears under the influence of suggestion. Why are physical sensations subject to psychic influence? We shall come to the conclusion that one element is the determining factor—Fire, which penetrates both the psychic and the physical domain. Even meningitis gives way under suggestion. This seemingly incurable affliction retreats before the power of Fire. Of course suggestion is first of all a fiery concentration. A man who causes such a fiery reaction thus calls forth a tension of the injured organs. Therefore the power of hypnotic suggestion must be greatly developed, but must be subject to state control. Something similar to the control over the Egyptian priests, who had the right to employ suggestion but who had to give full account of their actions in the temple assemblies.

41. Some children have a habit of breaking things in moments of leisure. Sometimes an ordinary plate may be broken, but sometimes with the same movement a precious cup may be destroyed. Therefore one must direct one's thought upon the most essential and refrain from all petty actions. The intent to inflict even a small harm is already criminal. At present, when we approach decisive events, there is no time to be occupied with trivial things. One must keep in mind that the most decisive time is at hand.

42. To turn to the future is not at all easy. It sounds simple—to leave the past and look to the future. It is both simple and beautiful, but how shall we light the bonfires of the past and where shall we find the fires to illumine the future? The attainment of the spirit will prompt how to find these boundaries and measures. But how to squeeze the heroic deed into everyday life? Fortunately every heart is a ready purse for achievement. In all times the population has been divided into settlers and nomads. The nomads moved by the power of search for achievement, they had no place of their own. But for the future they found the strength of achievement. Such striving of the heart is inherent in every human life. Amidst the precipitants resulting from heroic achievements must be found this noble restlessness, leading into the future. Only thus may one escape the snares of the past. I already have told you that one should avoid reminiscences in the Subtle World. They are like fetters! But already here one must become accustomed to the striving into the future. It is not said that one should not know the past; precisely knowledge is blessed. But one must not get stuck in the dust of the forefathers. Thus without forgetting, without limiting, let us advance towards the New Worlds. The freedom of consciousness gives birth to heroes. Discipline of spirit affirms the wise, and only the ignorant understand the future as a new bed. It is best to imagine movement and flights.

43. We may rejoice at transition into the Higher World, and the transition of the objects of creative art also represents such a step. Even such destruction is thus turned to benefit. There is the martyrdom of man, of animals and plants, and also the martyrdom of objects. The shortness of the path of martyrdom is evident everywhere. One may see these parallels in all kingdoms of Nature. The path of martyrdom, both bodily and spiritual, is the shortest. Martyrdom is called the Fiery Bridge. But during the battle one must utilize all possibilities. Thus you see both small and great circumstances.

44. I direct you into the future because of physical reasons also. One must not forget that in the Subtle World one can sense not only heat but also cold. Normally both sensations are unnecessary but they result from the bringing over of earthly, not yet outlived particles. The striving into the future is the best liberation from the earthly husks. Thus one may once more be convinced that thought carries with itself purely physical consequences. Of course, in the Subtle World it is necessary to get rid of earthly sensations. If they are felt, it means that some earthly particles threaten to impede the ascent. The Subtle World, when in harmony, does not give earthly sensations. Simply speaking, its denizens do not lose their energy through such sensations, which in the earthly state cause much overburdening. One may prepare the consciousness for liberation from all kinds of unnecessary survivals. For even upon Earth at certain reminiscences people exclaim, "I am flushed with heat! Cold pierces my heart!" But while upon Earth a thought may cause a sensory physical reaction, in the Subtle World this is true on a considerably greater scale. Only the future can liberate one from the burden of sensations. And it is not too difficult to accustom oneself to think about the future, if the striving to the Most High is already assimilated. Thus affirm in all actions the usefulness of the understanding of the future. Many remembrances, regrets, offenses and unnecessary things of the past only repulse the already formed magnetism of the future. The magnetism of the future is a great moving force, and it must be understood as absolute reality.

45. Actually the cycle of Aquarius already operates and coexists with the end of Pisces. Usually the beginning and end of a cycle is very gradual, and thus is affirmed the harmony of the actual evolutionary process. If there were sharp boundary lines between such original special factors, destruction and cataclysms would occur. And as it is, Aquarius has brought already a considerable shift of consciousness; but an increase would bring about a destructive revolution there where constructiveness is necessary. Even with an unprepared eye one may notice the alternate influence of Pisces and Aquarius. But humanity, which absolutely has not assimilated in its consciousness the understanding of this, must not be permitted to revolt.

46. The Earthly World in its essence is antagonistic to the Subtle World, because every chaotic state threatens subtle constructions. The same difference exists between the Subtle and the Fiery World, for the sediments of the former are not in the nature of Fire. Therefore every fiery thought receives an opposition from both the subtle and the earthly world. But one can conquer this condition only through fiery tension, because the fire of spirit is needed for the consuming of chaos and its transmutation. Fire is not directed there where reason tries to argue with chaos. The fire of the heart penetrates through chaos and transmutes it into a useful substance. The laboratory of the heart is powerful, and thought itself must be purified by Fire.

47. The application of psychic energy was differently pointed out in various Schools. Some proposed to strain the energy continuously, while others preferred to interrupt this current by repressing the energy into inaction. The two methods in their essence do not differ from each other, if the consciousness is developed. In an exalted state the energy receives continuous impulses, and when it seems to be inactive it is merely submerged into the depth of consciousness. Such seeming contrasts are manifested during inner concentration. Some believe that the uttering of certain words is essential, others directly transmit this mental action into the rhythm of the heart. The two ways are equally useful if the spirit is already elevated. During the elevation of the spirit one must maintain an even warmth of the heart. One must avoid shocks as unnecessary and harmful. One may become convinced that the heart can be in constant service to Hierarchy. With it the heart does not lose its responsiveness to all everyday questions. Such combination of contrasts does not alter the rhythm of the heart. I draw attention to the most everyday conditions because the Leader must deal with every mediator of life.

48. Some may ask why I speak of a Leader and not of a Ruler. The difference between them is enormous. The conception of Ruler presupposes the present and the ruling over something already existing, but the Leader manifests the future in the very significance of the word. He has not received anything already built; he leads, and each of his actions impels forward. The Ruler knows that which is already built and accomplished, but the Leader confronts nothing which is already affirmed and must bring the people to the

Mount of Perfection. If the burden of the Ruler is great, then the responsibility of the Leader is still greater, and therefore the Highest Powers affirm their Altar there, where there are signs of such Leadership. Precisely the Leader must discriminate between hypocrisy and sincerity. The manifestation of the virtue of the heart differs greatly from a forced servility. The Leader has the power to discern this quality.

Many have read how David interrogated the Highest Powers. He took recourse in this Source in order to avoid unnecessary errors. There are many such instances in the history of different nations. Everyone knows about them. It is not necessary to delve into the ancient times; these signs of Communion and Great Service are apparent in recent events. But we also know that for the High Communion a pure heart is needed. Nothing impure can partake of this Communion, therefore the symbol of the Leader must be the sign of purity of the heart. Not only in actions but in thoughts the Leader carries the welfare of the people. He knows that he is entrusted to bring a full chalice. He does not lose his path in useless wanderings. He will not spill the entrusted chalice. Thus the concept of the Leader is a sign of the future.

49. Useful reading is accompanied by sparks of radiance. The heart cannot remain silent to the joy of spirit. As they are needed the more varied are the signs.

50. Remember to what an extent people are in need of the concept of a Leader. They want to have someone who will be a Sponsor before the Highest. They understand how impossible it is to find the path without this link, but they know that the Leader comes. Nothing can ever impede the Leader if he is not held back by the earthly manifestations, which determine his retreat. The pure striving of the Leader cannot be stopped before the appointed time.

51. It is already known that a tremor of horror causes a contraction of the nerves of the skin at the nape of the neck. But people forget that the nerve substance of the spine sends a sort of arrow for restoration of the confused consciousness. One may think that the tremor at the back of the head is an expression of terror, but instead of that it is only a protective arrow.

52. There are many convulsions in the planet. The volcanic belt is shifting considerably. If solar spots influence earthly matters, no less do poisonous gases of an earthly shock have an effect. People do not sufficiently observe the effect of earthquakes upon human consciousness. Not only is the consciousness atremor near the centers of earthquakes, but also in space this effect is irradiated as a strong poisoning. Only the ignorant can say—"what have I to do with the gases in Chile or in Siberia?" Ignoramuses do not wish to think on a world scale, but everyone who already thinks of the Fiery World understands the significance of subterranean gases and of rays from beyond.

53. An invulnerable armor may be of metal or of silk, but the best armor is the fiery one. Can the Leader proceed by the ordained path without the fiery armor? With what other means may one deflect all arrows of malice and swords of hatred? But many Leaders even in their earthly consciousness have felt that they were protected by the fiery armor. Whole books can be written about the magnetism of the destined Leader. It may be observed that neither the outer appearance, nor the voice, nor riches, but something else convinces people. More than once have I spoken about the Fire of the heart. Precisely this armor is a magnet which attracts and protects. As it has been said, "I will receive all arrows in my shield." But this shield must be forged. This shield can be manifested only from Above. But how many thoughts and discourses must be sent in advance, in order that this Communion be established and the fiery armor forged! One should lose not a day nor an hour, to make the Communion living and ever-present. In error people think that science precludes the Higher World; it can alter earthly nomenclature, but the triune essence remains the basis. The more so does the Leader know wherein is the substance. Perhaps he will not express the Unutterable Word, but he will feel it in his heart. That Word will help the Leader not to lose the universal concept, only this will bring readily the wondrous armor.

54. Flammarion strains his thought toward the creation of the subtle body of a planet. And indeed the body of a planet is created by thought, but the conception of the planet proceeds not from the Subtle World, but from the Fiery. When the Fiery Seed has been formed, then the thought of the Subtle World can be also useful. A multitude of fiery seeds are whirling in space. A multitude of heavenly bodies are to be found already in the subtle aspect. Truly, space is not only filled but overcrowded. Thus the destruction of worlds, which is taking place every second, is only the actual generation of new bodies that have taken form. But it is correct to understand that this germination requires a fiery thought. Strive toward the Fiery World in order to participate in the higher creativeness. It is a mistake to think that it is inaccessible. Precisely every developed consciousness should strive toward the joy of creativeness. This striving already in itself is the beginning of cooperation. Though the thought of Flammarion cannot give a fully complete result, this thought is vast, noble and deserves our rejoicing over it. He constantly strived towards the broadening of understanding. Thus even his errors took on an aspect of usefulness; besides he did not allow his mind to wither, and was able to leave the Earth still young in spirit. In the Subtle World, while some ignorant ones try to think about murder the scientist dreams about a beautiful creation.

55. An example of the opposite is when the mind has been withered through non-understanding of the Teaching—then one may reply, "It is enough to whine over your offences, you have had ample time to broaden your consciousness, you could have observed the heavenly worlds and understood the Source of the Teachings; but instead of this you wish to carry away with you earthly offences. What is the Teaching and Wisdom of the ages to you, when your thoughts instead of expanding have been shrunk in offence? No one has insulted you, but you have offended yourself."

Thus in the Subtle World small thoughts are crowded. One may regret that so much energy is wasted in quarrels and mutual belittling. But if it be asked to what extent such thoughts of the Subtle World are chemically harmful, one can only say that small unkind thoughts generate poisonous gases. One must think not of oneself, but to what an extent people may harm each other even in the Subtle World. But every kind thought and striving towards the Beautiful helps one to advance rapidly.

56. The thought-will remains the only basis of the All-existence, therefore the energy of the thought must be so carefully investigated.

57. You will find people who will say—Away with Leaders, away with Teachers, away with Guides! Be assured that they are parasites who feed upon turmoil and decay. Falsehood and oppression lie in the nature of these parasites. Secretly they hoard riches, and are not averse to reaping luxury. Thus one should discern all those who are builders by nature, and those who are destroyers. Thus it is right to abide with those who know the joy of labor. They also know the Guiding Powers and they reverence the Teacher, for their nature is directed toward cooperation.

58. Verily miracles do occur, and it is worth while to live in cognizance of miracles. A great many ready combinations are shattered by blunt denials and by shameful blindness of consciousness.

59. Education in the primary schools and secondary schools must be the same for both sexes. It is inadmissible to impose upon a child some specialty, when it is not yet able to define its own aptitude. It is sufficient to begin in high school to map out programs according to students' abilities. Thus one may plan the education of children who cannot yet express their inherent capabilities. It is very important that the program should not differ for the two sexes. This alone will eliminate a very harmful attitude towards sex.

60. To direct the consciousness into the future is the aim of a true school. Few seem to understand that the projecting of the consciousness into the future is the formation of a guiding magnet. But what matters is that the consciousness should be fully directed into the future. Many seem to think that they may sometimes ponder about the future, and then again dive into the past. Not isolated thoughts should be allotted to the future, but the essence of consciousness should be attuned in the key of the future. It is impossible to force oneself to such transformation. One can attain only by growing to love the future. But not many love the future. The country of the joy of labor, in perfecting the quality of labor, can be naturally drawn into the future. The duty of the Leader is to direct the people into the future.

61. The art of thinking must be developed in schools. Every art is in need of exercise. Likewise thinking must be strengthened by practice. But such a deepening should not be burdensome nor tedious, therefore the instructor in such a subject must be truly enlightened. It may be seen that the most terrible calamities in the history of mankind have arisen from the inability to think. There may be found a multitude of examples wherein spasmodic thinking and unbridled feelings have led whole nations towards the abyss. On the other hand, laziness of thinking and slow-mindedness have destroyed accumulated possibilities. The Leader must provide in himself the example of a constant broadening of thinking in order to approach foresight. Of course, foresight results from Communion with Hierarchy. But Communion itself requires alertness in thinking and a clear striving. The art of thinking should not be understood as an occult concentration. There is nothing mysterious in the art of thinking and in the refinement of consciousness. Only a lofty quality of consciousness will affirm the path of the thinker. And no one will say that the thinker is a special genus. Every child can be directed towards thinking. Hence, one must regard the art of thinking as the health of the nation.

62. The evolutionary world processes must be very attractively presented in schools. A motherland is the result of world processes and must occupy a fully defined place and significance. Everyone must know the true value of his country, but it must not be a tree growing in the wilderness. It has to cooperate with many nations. Also, a belief in the Higher Justice will come from the knowledge of reality. Let the processes of the World find vivid interpreters. Care must be taken that these great paths of nations be not distorted for the sake of ignorance.

63. Every unification can take place only on a cooperative basis. To admit but an element of conquest, suppression and humiliation, means that sooner or later these horrible shadows will turn into destructive monsters. Therefore no act of violence can enter into the construction of the Stronghold. One may find the power of joy in cooperation, but such cooperation requires the art of thinking. Who will distribute the forces for productive labor? Only he who is able to visualize a useful cooperation. He must know how to imagine such labor in common, but, as you know, imagination must be cultivated. The task of every school is the opening of a well-founded imagination.

64. Correct is the consideration about mediums that their lymph is a mechanical link with the Astral World. But, limited to mechanics, mediumism is not protected against outside intrusion. It is also correct to understand that the forces of darkness exert all their ingenuity to remain in earthly spheres.

65. One may notice even during daytime a feeling as of absence. One should very attentively observe this state. It shows that partially the subtle body has left for distant work. One may feel dizziness and tension in the center of the Brahmarandra. This results from a partial presence of the subtle body which is subjected to special pressure of the fiery seed. One should not strain oneself during this condition. It is useful to sit awhile quietly with closed eyes. One also may mentally send currents to the subtle body which is at work. Furthermore, one should not burden oneself with geography nor distance, but should send a quiet bidding to the toiling subtle body. One must not tire oneself when so many currents are tensed. Not only are heavy currents fatiguing, but a reinforced sending of success can be a burden. Blows upon the aura may be from the most varied causes. Not in vain did the ancient priests cover the heart with the left hand—as with a lightning rod—because the fingers strongly repulse the blows.

66. One must not think that the sounds of the far-off worlds will be something hard to imagine. First of all they will resound, because the current creates vibration. One should accustom oneself to such sounds. One may understand that the so-called music of the spheres rather often comparatively borders on the sounding of the far-off worlds. In any case, every music of the spheres is already a bond between the worlds, because this vibration reaches unaltered the most distant planets.

67. One must pay attention to the origins of various epidemics. The manifestation of this or that epidemic is reflected upon the general conscious forces. The poisoning penetrates deeper than one may think, and regenerates and creates new microbes. Physical and psychic epidemics are very pernicious. Many degenerations of entire families originate from such regenerated microbes.

68. Do not overeat, in other words be circumspect in food. Illnesses can especially develop when the manifestations of difficult currents are evident. One may observe the diseases of plants and animals also, and note that their healing can become difficult. Thus not only human illnesses, but the maladies of the whole world should attract the attention of scientists.

69. Certain insects and reptiles choose to perish, only to be able to bite and release their poison. Similarly, the servitors of darkness are ready for the most disagreeable consequences, if only they may create poisonous evil. One must firmly remember these creators of evil, who often do not spare even themselves for an evil deed. Many instances can be revealed of the carrying out nevertheless under the suggestions of the dark ones of a premeditated evil that could not be advantageous to the evil doer himself. The devices of the dark ones must be exposed. For example, sometimes one finds in the vicinity of certain places corpses of some people or animals. The dark ones know that for the attraction of the forces of the lower spheres decomposition is necessary, and they ingeniously arrange such centers of confusion and decay. For this reason I have for long advised not to keep in the house decomposing meat and decayed plants, nor stagnant water. People seldom pay attention to such dangers, which are confirmed even by our contemporary physicians.

70. Man must always be on the threshold of the future. Man is new every moment. Man cannot affirm himself upon the past, because it does not exist any longer. Man can know the past, but woe to him if he wants to apply the measures of the past. The past is incompatible with the future. The wisdom of the realization of new combinations unites the past with the future. It is not easy to know constantly and courageously that each moment renovates the worlds, but out of this source is born inexhaustible vigor. A council of wise men can convene, but let him who is senile in spirit, who has turned his face to the past, not come there. The light of the future is the Light of Hierarchy.

71. Bribery must be eradicated by all means, but one cannot rely upon punitive measures. They help little. In the lessons in Ethics in schools the thought must be affirmed that bribery does not conform to the dignity of man. One should observe very attentively whether such symptoms of corruption are making their appearance. Next to bribery in shamefulness is the nonfulfillment of duty. But this crime is assimilated so early that one can only counteract it by beginning from childhood. Let children get used to the work of grownups. The quality of labor will create the realization of duty. Every negligence, forgetfulness and evasion can be condemned only in one's own heart.

72. Verily courage is created through the indissoluble link with the Hierarchy. Courage can be contained in the seed and never reveal itself as armor of Light. But when our consciousness is completely transported into the domain where there is no fear and depression, then we are invulnerable to any filth. One should understand where lies one's strength, and should hasten thither without any evasiveness. Thus can courage be made firm.

73. People usually make the mistake of assuming, due to limitation of consciousness, that an object can exist in only one aspect. Therefore they cannot conceive that in ancient times people could avail themselves of various energies but applied them quite differently. People also forget that they themselves, when moving from their dwelling places, destroy many objects. So, too, the wise Teachers took measures for a timely concealment of that which was not to be revealed before its appointed time. Can new discoveries be given out before the appointed date? The very foundations could be shattered by such arbitrary attempts. Does not the Hierarchy participate in all discoveries? Do you not know that many discoveries have been destroyed as harmful because of their untimeliness? The Guiding Hand untiringly watches the current of possibilities for the Good.

74. Long ago it was known that people may become

acquainted in person or in thought. The latter affirmation is also useful at present.

75. Excessive heat and fire are raging, reminding us that before wars and upheavals conflagrations are prevalent.

76. Verily luxury must leave the new constructive order, the more so since luxury is akin neither to beauty nor to knowledge. But sinuous are the boundary lines of luxury. It is impossible to define them by one law. One must completely eradicate every vulgarity, which is the fellow-traveler of luxury.

77. In order to stimulate the cognizance of beauty in schools, let there be introduced a study of the beauty of life. The history of arts and sciences will enter into this subject, for it must not only embrace conceptions of the past, but also contain indications of contemporary achievement. The instructor in this subject must be truly enlightened, in order to avoid bigotry, which contains in itself the seed of ignorance.

78. The World lives in mystery, and the Highest Mystery is unrevealable. Similarly, in every tension there is an element of mystery. People sense in their hearts the boundary of this Mystery and are capable of respecting it. One must not invent mystery, but one must respect it. In this will lie justification of the human personality.

79. One may warn that every conscious contact with the forces of the Subtle World can be dangerous. When a subtle being seeks instructions from an earthly inhabitant the intentions are questionable, because in the Subtle World it is easy to find lofty Instruction.

80. To those who cannot accept the concept of the Leader, let us say: All your words presuppose the priority of something or someone. You yourself do not notice that each of your affirmations is based upon a discovery of something established by someone. There is no man who can get along without being taught. One must not become proud in one's own heart. The understanding of Hierarchy will help to establish the manifestation of the Leader, who in relation to the Higher Ones is not a leader but a follower. People, under the influence of ignorance, try sometimes to cut the ropes, but any sailor will tell you that masts are cut down when the elements overcome human strength. The same sailor knows that without masts and ropes the voyage is catastrophic. This means that the unavoidableness of Hierarchy throughout the Universe should be affirmed through education.

81. At the approach of great dates unprecedented tensions are unavoidable. The guiding and coordination of events are enormously difficult because of the poisoning of certain strata of the atmosphere. Some events ripen, as fruit under the scorching rays of the sun, but others grow mouldy, as stored things in damp weather. Remember that one cannot defer the dates. Such violation may cause cosmic cataclysms. Everyone must act according to his capacity, keeping in mind the Great Service.

82. Fiery sparks from flint remind us of the sparks of tension. During the crucial moments of the battle there may be blows which produce a multitude of sparks. The nearest ones can feel better than others such fiery streams, when they are drawn into the very battle. When I advise caution it means that the attacks are strong or the battle itself produces tension. The attacks first of all react upon the developed centers. One cannot avoid such influences. The saints suffered precisely from such tensions. But the most difficult has also its happy possibility. Precisely, the tension of battle or the suffering from attacks better than anything else refines the centers. Therefore, every one proceeding in the Great Service welcomes such tension as Wings of Light. One may feel that the upper part of the spinal column fairly groans under pressure, but this is the bearing of the earthly burden called the Burden of Atlas. One may advise physicians to pay more attention to the centers and to the heart.

83. Everyone summoning his neighbor to the fiery baptism is already a participant in the Great Service. Everyone accepting a part in the carrying of the Cross of Truth will not weaken. Everyone who has understood the needs of the World has shortened his path of ascent. Everyone who realizes the significance of the heart as the Abode of Agni is already upon the true path.

84. The verbal command remains in life, although humanity has at its disposal thousands of written languages. For this there are three reasons. First, the command is not always renderable in writing; second, people pay little attention when relying on writing; third, the manifestation of the Highest Teachings is never recorded in writing—therefore the lips whisper from heart to heart the highest commands. These considerations, though simple, require recording, for if someone does not know Hierarchy, he will not understand the sacredness of the Command. Many instructions about the laws of Nature are needed, in order to understand the entire beauty of the law of attraction which lies at the foundation of Hierarchy. Ignorant people do not understand that slavery dwells in darkness while freedom dwells in the Light of Hierarchy.

85. Verily the esteem for the spirit will grow. Godlessness must be eradicated. The fact is that it is better to preserve even fragments of the cognizance of Hierarchy, even in conventional forms, than to be cast into the abyss of chaos. When people heard about the unattainability of the Highest they began to reject in general everything Invisible. Therefore by My command godlessness, which has assumed the aspect of most obvious satanism, will be adjudged. One cannot tolerate any longer such involution.

86. Many criminals will turn to labor under suggestion. Just as drunkenness and other vices, ailments of crime may be cured by the command of the will. It must not be forgotten also that many crimes are committed under the influence of obsession. Consequently such people need to be cured, and not punished. Definitely, during such treatments, increased, systematic labor has a decisive significance; for the obsessing entities every labor is hateful. They try to cast one into chaos, but the essence of labor is already a counter-manifestation. One ought not be distressed by the thought as to whence will come the strong suggestions. They are many, but they are dissociated. When the Institute of Psychic Energy will be established, it will bring together many useful co-workers. It should not be forgotten that an Institute of Astrology would be very helpful toward the verification of data. Not long ago governments were ashamed to pay attention to heavenly luminaries, as well as to human powers, but psychic energy must occupy the attention of enlightened people.

87. Not without reason do people recall ancient prophecies about changes in the firmament. In fact, violation of the planet's equilibrium will cause many three-fold manifestations. Not only may new heavenly bodies become visible, but the very chemism of the Luminaries may be altered, and of course this will react strongly upon the inhabitants of Earth. Thus, while people are enjoying their bazaars and fairs, ominous

events are in the offing. Therefore one must undeferrably reiterate about the Living Ethics. The Sacred Ethics is transformed into a foolish etiquette and has become a printed label.

88. The science of atmospheric influences must undergo considerable changes. One may notice in contemporary apparatus unexplainable tremors which seemingly do not conform to other indications. Such traces of astral whirls bring to the Earth very significant effects. Besides, in this way are affirmed the relations with the Subtle World. Indeed, among the tensions of the Subtle World there may be such pressures that their reverberation even agitates manifested matter. First of all such waves are reflected upon the fiery centers. You yourself could observe how, despite the cool weather, the centers gave indication of great pressure. One must compare this with the reaction to the distant events, which also call forth vibrations of strong tensions. But the astral whirls are observed even less than telepathy. Scientists are unwilling to admit that in their physical considerations a factor of the world beyond can have any significance. But the effect of such whirls sometimes is almost equal to that of a bolt of lightning. I will not conceal the fact that strong cooling currents have had to be applied in order to counteract the reaction to such whirls. We stand on guard, and are ready to send rays, but the pressure of the currents of the Subtle World is unprecedented. They are fighting with the forces of darkness and one must have imagination in order to picture to oneself the magnitude of this battle.

89. The Leader must always be alert, in order that no one receive from him emanations of depression. But such alertness may be established only when devotion to Hierarchy is present, when the communion has entered the heart. From such Source proceeds magnanimity, which opens the most difficult gates. One must have before oneself the Image of the Hierarch, in order to find in all cases a basis of friendliness. One must know the Fiery Sword of the Archangel, in order to know the boundary of justice. Who can say when all measures of magnanimity are exhausted? The Hierarch alone can take upon himself such a decision.

90. One cannot appoint for responsible positions people who are embittered. One must guard very carefully against such a quality, because embitterment is a limitation. Of course limitation, up to a certain extent, can be cured, as can embitterment. Both qualities yield to suggestion, but such transformation requires time. A terrible harm results from embitterment. It imprints itself as an unsurmountable obstacle upon all actions of a man who has succumbed to it.

91. In the approach to the Fiery World one has to pass the step of repulsion of the dark forces by the power of the spirit. A man who ascends feels much more deeply the assault of the unbridled elements. He must, without resorting to magic's violations, withstand the assault of the dark ones by his own spirit alone. This step is mentioned in all Teachings under different names. One must be prepared to meet various crafty devices, but one should not, taking the example of ignorant ones, try to escape such unavoidable encounters. One may remember that above all formulas there exists the power of the spirit. One has but to unite it, through one's heart, with the Hierarch, in order to become invulnerable. It must not be thought that one can be forsaken by the Hierarch, but it must be remembered that on a certain step independent application of one's strength is primarily advised. Thus, one should face each assault courageously, not avoiding the most terrifying. Remember that every retreat manifests helplessness. Even the youngest neophytes know that during necessary changes of place one must move facing the enemy. This is not magic, but only the realization of the power of the gaze.

92. It should be remembered that the New Firmament can become visible. Quite some time ago I mentioned that a new heavenly body is approaching, but as yet it is concealed from observation. It must not be forgotten that the energy radiated by humanity is necessary for the proper motion of the planet. But when this energy becomes poisoned it weakens the protective net of the planet and thus upsets the equilibrium of many luminaries. The waves of vibrations are altered and the planet loses part of its self-defense. Thus humanity itself is master of its own destiny. But when there comes the destructive period of so-called godlessness, then the mass of energy which is usually sent into the higher layers is shattered and becomes the material for the brown gas.

93. Humanity does not wish to realize the power of its own radiations. It dimly keeps on repeating about its likeness to God, but does not understand the unity of the energy of all worlds. The establishment of even a weak unification of energy can provide a defensive armor for the planet.

94. The heart in its full significance is a transmuter and a condenser. Often these processes happen to be so strong that human strength cannot suffice to contain and endure the tension. From antiquity has come the prayer about resigning one's spirit to God. One should understand truly this surrender of the spirit. If you feel an unbearable anguish of the heart, transfer it mentally to the Lord. Thus you may join your heart with the Inexhaustible Source—Hierarchy. Such action may be particularly needed when the tension of the entire planet is great. One must be prepared for the most diversified influences, both cosmic and human. The adherence of the heart to Hierarchy is a continuous action, but at present We are pointing out particular instances when it becomes necessary to strengthen the heart with the manifestation of Hierarchy with especial clarity of consciousness. Many will not understand how one can strengthen the heart by thought, because for them the heart is but a physical organ. But whoever has felt Our currents will understand the meaning of this bond. The World is living through such tension that it is timely to remind about the necessity of readiness for such communions. The Fiery World must be evoked in full consciousness. In case of need one may even orally address the Lord. Upon all steps of Hierarchy there is the same transmission and communion. And how majestic is this Ladder of Immeasurable Help.

95. The rhythm of events often cannot be conceived by many, and in this I am including not only those of mankind, but also of Nature. Sudden climatic sharp variations do not attract the attention of people, but such revolts cannot be stopped by the secret police. Yet they do take place and act upon the brain. Of course We know about the life of ideas which cannot be stopped by any generation, but people do not believe in ideas!

96. The realization of Higher Forces is not taught in schools, nor given from outside, but it lives precisely in the heart, being the very cornerstone of the remembrance of life in the Subtle World. One may say—be blessed, you who have preserved in your heart the most Beautiful. The clouding of humanity comes from forgetting that which is most needed. Night is given for the upliftment of the spirit, but man has said in his ignorance that sleep is like death. It is absurd to compare a wondrous mystery with dissolution. One must reiterate from childhood on that sleep is communion with Angels. When words are unnecessary, then begins the realization through the heart.

97. Surveillance must be very vigilant, but it must not appear as a sign of mistrust. One must transform control into cooperation and reciprocal information. Measures of trust and refinement of quality must be introduced from top to bottom. Many useful measures have been condemned and destroyed only because of hatred of supervision. Of course ignorance is the cause of such lack of goalfitness. When people will become cognizant of the Subtle and Fiery Worlds, they will comprehend the infinity of relationships. In truth, who is outside of Hierarchy? Only ignoramuses or conscious deceivers can render Hierarchy unintelligible under various names. But they themselves will breathe not the freedom of Hierarchy, but will bear the brand of slavery. One must be cleansed of all covetousness and bondage. From early childhood the freedom of discipline of spirit should be emphasized. One may arouse all dignity and honor. Without honor a man cannot be honest. It should not be thought that slavery can be approved by Hierarchy. On the contrary, the Fiery World seeks not slaves but co-workers. Consider the refinement of the heart as the measure of honor. Thus let us not forget that in the most everyday life are laid the foundations of the world's grandeur.

98. One must manifest care about Hierarchy. Hierarchy is not despotism, but the Stronghold of Love. Only out of love is born the reverence which creates discipline. But few love the one who helps them. It means that ignorance is great.

99. If it is difficult sometimes to concentrate thought, also it is not easy sometimes to get rid of thought. However, this quality also must be attained. Physicians have noticed haunting thoughts. Such a state can be the result not only of obsession, but also of inertia of the brain centers. One must know how to set aside, as it were, a useless intrusive thought.

To this end one may perform little exercises, forcing oneself to consciously put aside a thought, as if massaging the brain. Many people fail to understand at all what We are talking about, but such immobility of the brain must be routed by different tasks, so that a preceding thought in no way colors the following one. Such a coloring usually deprives the new formations of preciseness.

100. When you observe nagging thoughts, you may notice that usually they are of the most everyday nature. They may be called a product of the Earth, but in spite of their small significance, they attempt to contend with the greatest ideas. One should carefully cleanse the brain of these unbidden guests. Indeed, there is a time for everything. One may be making all progress, but it should be remembered that small worms may succeed in boring through a very strong tree. Particularly do they love to undermine the anchor of confidence. Beside mistrust, one may also admit obscuring thoughts. It is terrible to lose confidence—it is almost like the loss of communion. When suddenly, instead of communion, a mute emptiness breaks in, this is surely an abyss!

101. It is correct to remove from one's home all rotting substances. But besides decomposition of meat and water, equally harmful are decaying fruit and wilting flowers. When someone takes measures for the removal of dead flowers, one may observe that straight-knowledge removes lifeless plants not only in the name of beauty, but through knowledge of the law of the Subtle World. Since lower entities feed upon decomposition, then for lack of putrid products they are satisfied with plants. He can be commended whose spirit whispers the correct attitude toward all surroundings.

102. In contrast with confidence there is depression. Precisely distrust begets this awful viper. But trust awakens the most fiery, the most divine instincts of the spirit. Beings of the Fiery World can approach people in hours of trust, and the miracle of enthusiasm creates the most beautiful approaches. Trust must be cultivated, as otherwise people sink into inertia. Trust is straight-knowledge; there can be no betrayal when we know the direction of our striving. We rejoice when approaching a man who guards the fire of trust. Many beautiful creations take place when the gates of trust are open, gates purified by Fire.

103. When cities were enumerated to you where the ritual of black magic was especially developed, it did not mean that there were no other places where it could be found. On the contrary, there are many black lodges, but some of them are devoted to evil as such, without any special rituals. But during recent times one may see a revival of the most ancient services of darkness. Among them there are very harmful ones, which can cause destruction by their very rhythm. The black lodges usually do not understand what cosmic harm they create. In their ignorance they think that they cause harm only in a desired direction, but in reality they touch whole strata of the atmosphere. Especially at present, when the fiery time is approaching and there are already evident many violations of the equilibrium, the harm of the evocations of the

dark ones is particularly frightful. The ignorant act here also, by manifest destructions.

104. Black lodges must be destroyed very carefully. The fact is that they do not exist as oasis only, but are infiltrated into apparently the most respectable circles. That is why it is difficult to eradicate evil. But people who consider themselves to be on the side of Light do not give sufficient aid, because they lack trust, not having developed it. One may name cases of direct betrayal which people regarded as trust, so confused are the concepts.

105. If on entering a house you noticed a viper on the host's table, what would you do? Would you think the matter over, while the snake attacked your friend, or would you decide at once to crush it? We say—save your friend from evil. Do not becloud your head with perplexity, but act for the good. One cannot put on the same scale a man and a snake. It is impossible to put on the same level the lower consciousness and the temple of consciousness. If we cease to discriminate, where will be our responsibility before the world? He is no hero who spares the snake and loses a friend. Not a hero is he who evades his duty while offering excuses. Not a hero is he who does not distinguish between the great and the small. Not a hero is he who has lost the measuring rod of the heart. The Leader knows the heart measure and the fiery solution.

106. Let us approach the most difficult, before which all former difficulties will appear as blissful moments. The most difficult is the blessing of the Fiery World. This entry is so difficult that it seems that not even our minutest cell can endure this World of ecstasy. It has been said that when all covering has fallen away and only the radiance of daring remains, then the resplendent Fire enters the Gates, there being no admittance for the body. But in order to kindle such daring, let us preserve ecstasy in the face of the most difficult. Therefore reflect, the way you would wish to imagine existence in the Fiery World. Indeed, thought creates in the Subtle World, but it is quick as lightning in the Fiery World, and transcends all earthly measures; there is the Seventh Light.

107. The Seventh Light is the most containing; therefore each earthly containment will already be a path thither, where each spirit is alight with radiance. The destruction of containment and rapture imposes the chief obstacle to rapid advancement. One must learn about the existence of the Hierarchy of Worlds which is infinite. Let children at least receive an allusion to the beauty of Infinity. At first will be uttered the word, but later will be born the concept. The manifestation of the Fiery World brings a beautiful rapture.

108. The most perfect machine can be stopped by the smallest stone; the more refined the machine the more sensitive it will be to any foreign body. Is not this very same thing true of the heart? Therefore it is essential to guard the current of the heart. When the current strives upward myriads of small sendings rush forth to impede it. Not only conscious and malicious sendings but also chaotic particles move to restrain the rising current. But if we are aware of it our consciousness will not admit the unbidden guests. In small and in great one must be on guard, so that enemies may not cut the current. Even a small distrust or regret takes away a degree of the current. Besides, there is another harm. When a contact has been established, the deviation of one degree makes also the higher current uneven. It must be understood that such a violation of currents is dangerous in many respects. All nerve centers react to these currents. Each fluctuation destroys the labor of several centers. Therefore it is necessary to regard cautiously the currents of the heart.

109. Relativity expands into Infinity—there is the same law for knowledge. No one in the Worlds can be satisfied with his knowledge. New acquisitions increase progressively the realization of lack of knowledge. The faint-hearted may become frightened before the infinitude of knowledge, but we already know the inevitability of this law, and we labor daily so as to rejoice at this infinitude.

110. Joy at achievement is a shield of beauty. You already know how abysses have been crossed through joy and trust. Likewise one must rejoice at the next approaching achievement. Not only courage, but precisely joy makes you invulnerable. Even great achievements have been simplified through joy and trust.

111. One can draw slight comparison between the Fiery World and the earthly. During the rare manifestations of the Beings of the Fiery World, they take all measures not to violate earthly equilibrium, and the earthly people, for their part, at the approach of such Beings take measures to protect the heart. But with all protective measures, the heart often cannot endure the fiery tension—thus the higher measures from above and below cannot join these Worlds. The rarest cases of communion can be attributed to old karma, when during earthly lives lengthy cooperations for good took place. Such cooperations are useful for eternity. The establishing of an association consolidates collaboration. When our gaze is directed into the future, each benevolent cooperation constitutes a wise action.

112. One can intensify one's will by the most mechanical expedients. Many examples and prescriptions can testify to this, but We advise to gather the strengthening of the will from Communion with

Hierarchy. It may even be said that in general this is the sole means of the ascent of the spirit. Even the path of mechanics leads to the same thing, but through useless expenditures of time and effort. The communion with Hierarchy through the heart releases one from tantras and magic. Naturally, small alien hindrances can harm the communion, but let us not forget to what dangers the magician or the tantrik are exposed. But, in any case, he is not wise who dreams about his own separate will; it grows and vibrates in the Higher Treasuries. And he who is concerned about his individual will, without the communion with the Higher Worlds, is not on the true path.

113. In order to reestablish the forgotten Hierarchy one should accept its goalfitness from all sides, from the highest to the lowest. Thus one may avoid the usual error of people who seemingly have already recognized Hierarchy but immediately repudiate it at the slightest inconvenience to them. Such violations hinder greatly the implantation of a new consciousness.

114. It has been correctly observed about the final test through fear; after irritation, doubt, temptations have been passed, there remain the horrors of the lower strata. But after the strengthening of the communion with Hierarchy these disgusting spectacles do not any more affect the hearts. One can even rejoice at the attempts to dismay one, since these are already at the final boundary.

115. If people were able to draw an account of the quality of a day, they could avoid many difficulties. Indeed, astrology is a very exact science, and it demands extremely accurate correlation. It is evident that astrological data is limited to place and time. This is quite comprehensible when we picture a plan of intersecting currents. Thus, above all possible inaccuracies of our astrological interpretations, there exists the great indicator—the heart. The two sources must be unified. Let the most exact calculations of astrology be united with the heart. The heart will tell in its own silent language where is the hardship which must be outlived, or the joy which must be utilized. But let the wisdom of the heart not be turned into superstition, and let the tablet of the astrologer not become a dried skeleton. A great number of petty circumstances vibrate in space, and only the fiery heart can understand the invisible network of causes. The Rays of the Luminaries intersect nations, races, individuals. One may recognize the immutability of the chemism of the constellations, but the analysis of such diverse confluence must be very carefully interpreted. The heart can assist, but even in straight-knowledge it is guided by Hierarchy. With justice people turn to the science of astrology, but without the fiery heart they may find themselves in an impassable jungle. Thus let us remember the heart, otherwise speaking, the Hierarchy.

116. Actually, the very highest magic is as naught before the face of the Fiery World. One may convince oneself that magic is able to contend with the dark forces, but Fiery Beings are unexpected even by the higher magic. You esteem St. Sergius, but did He ever admit magic? He did not even employ inner concentration, nevertheless He did have flaming visions. He admitted only work, as an exaltation of the heart. In this, He outdistanced many spiritual wayfarers. We speak about the heart, but precisely He found the strength of this source. Even terrors were allayed by Him not through conjurations but by the prayer of the heart.

117. Inner concentration is a great thing, but nothing should be limited. Infinity itself points to inexhaustible Light. One may count the contents of man's every cell and be amazed at the immeasurableness of space. Thus one should turn to the Source, which is not awed by Infinity itself. Such is the spark contained in the heart. Neither physician, nor builder, nor scholar, can dispense with the straight-knowledge of the heart.

118. Labor may be of four kinds—toil with repulsion, which leads to decomposition; unconscious toil, which does not strengthen the spirit; toil devoted and loving, which yields a good harvest; and finally, toil which is not only conscious but also consecrated under the Light of Hierarchy. The ignorant may suppose that uninterrupted communion with Hierarchy can distract one from striving for the work itself, but, on the contrary, constant communion with Hierarchy lends a higher quality to one's labor. Only the eternal Source deepens the significance of perfectionment. This flaming measure of labor must be established. The very approach to the Fiery World demands realization of earthly labor as the most proximate step. Few of the workers can discern the quality of their own work, but if the worker were to strive to Hierarchy, he would immediately advance to a higher step. The ability to establish the sacred Hierarchy in one's heart is also an inner concentration, but such action comes through toil. By not wasting time upon oneself, it is possible in the midst of labor to become linked to Hierarchy. Let the Lord live in the heart. Let Him become as inalienable as the heart itself. Let the Name of the Lord be inhaled and exhaled with each breath. Let each rhythm of labor resound with the Name of the Lord. Thus should each one who thinks about the Fiery World know how to conduct himself. Can I lie before the Lord? Can I conceal anything from the

Lord? Can I contemplate treason in the presence of the Lord Himself? Thus let each reflection only strengthen and restrain one from the evil of faintheartedness and dark thoughts.

119. Know how to make use of each action around you, in order to make light in the darkness. Who, then, will not awaken when abominable roarings violate the equilibrium of the planet? One should remember whence the darkness comes creeping. At first the appearance of bandits calls forth a shout, but then man moves to protect his labor and everything beautiful connected with it. The dead remain silent, but even silence can store up energy.

120. When slavery, the shame of the World, is manifested, then one must expect a change of epoch. Can one expect the advent of Maitreya to be possible only in four hundred thousand years? Many times has confusion been caused by mere words. It is impossible to imagine the Earth submerged in darkness for another thousand of years. Just picture the progression of evil! Therefore the most fierce Armageddon can be regarded as salvation. The wise cannot but feel an anguish of the spirit.

121. The World is moulded in beautiful Principles. The expression about the renunciation of the World is incorrect. One cannot renounce the heavenly beauty. The whole World has been given to man. Therefore it would be far truer to speak about the discovery of the meaning of things. When the manifestation of renunciation arises, it concerns the most perverted concepts, the most harmful actions, but it is inadmissible to misuse a beautiful concept, the World, to describe a generalization of these abominations of ignorance. Worldly matters do not have to be unworthy and shameful. Great consciousnesses have taken great pains over the

World. It is unfitting to attribute to them the distortions of ignorance! In studying the foundations of the Fiery World, it is first of all necessary to have an agreement over the understanding of many concepts. Is it at all possible to call gluttony, or depravity, or theft, or betrayal, Worldly matters? They are even beneath the actions of animals. Animals know the measure of need, but if man has forgotten the measure of justice it is only because he has abandoned the World and has fallen into darkness. Whoever does not reflect more worthily about the World, is not able to distinguish right from wrong. How could he comprehend the Blessed Fire? He would shudder at the very thought of the Fiery World. Let us advise friends to gradually differentiate the World from chaos. I advise friends to begin discourses about the fiery element as the subject of forthcoming revelations.

122. The appearance of spots on Saturn only indicates cosmic ruptures, which are sending an unprecedented chemism to the Earth. There are many similar manifestations about which scholars even decide not to speak. The forces of space are restless; one need not think that a cataclysm will be just tomorrow, but one may realize that new chemisms are approaching the sick planet.

123. Achievement of the spirit is opposed to the forces of chaos. One may rejoice when even a sign of achievement draws near. One may rejoice when the Teacher indicates the possibility of an achievement.

124. New planetary chemisms have an enormous significance. One may picture that the chemism of Saturn is attracting a certain type of being. Who knows what penalty is being prepared for those who serve Satan? You have long known the old legend about Satan. One must note that the fury of those who serve him already reaches the point of madness. Thus, for some the spot on Saturn is just a spot, but for others it is a confirmation of the old legend. Many manifestations are related to Armageddon.

125. Many precious concepts have been perverted. When I say, "Be not too much concerned about tomorrow," this does not mean that I am advising you to be a sluggard. All thinking must be directed into the future; one should labor for the future, but one's care about the sacred future ought to be directed through Hierarchy. Then one's thought about tomorrow will assume proper consideration. Fear of the morrow is like amputation of hands and feet. Instead of flight into the future, people bind themselves with fear and stop their own movement. But without Hierarchy one can actually plunge into terror, as if sinking into a stormy ocean. Thus, the care, purified by Hierarchy, will not be an earthly one, though it will preserve action and usefulness. Besides, such consecrated usefulness is freed from any egoism. The care for the Common Welfare leads to communion with Hierarchy. Again, this judgment is not abstract ethics, but the path to the Fiery World. People in the earthly state also should select each seed which will grow into a plant for the thread of communion. It is not easy for Fiery Beings to penetrate into the earthly strata. Ought we not, while here, pierce through the carnate garments with our consciousness? There are many striving ones, but few are strengthened by the straight-knowledge drawn from Hierarchy.

126. Let us ponder to what extent obedience is merely a cooperation. The collaboration which is extended into the Highest Abodes is not a burden. To be sure, fanatics will suspect pride in such infinite striving, but the fanatic's head, in any position, touches the same great Infinity. Thus one may advise fanatics to beware of superstition. Therefore let us not be confused by such voices, and let us be strengthened upon the concept of Hierarchy as the most vital Principle.

127. We speak here about the Highest Principle. But just now things of the lowest order are being created in the world. Thus one can see madness of whole nations. Right now six wars are going on, but people do not see them. Right now evil is being accumulated like an explosive substance. But people do not notice the volcano. Even the wisest rulers are not terrified by these manifestations, considering that somehow all will be well.

128. A renewal of energies is required in everything. The most powerful manifestations are in need of higher currents. Schools have the task of developing in students the understanding of the unity of the elements. It has been thought that the composition of the air is the same everywhere. People have thought like this up to the present, otherwise they would have taken suitable measures. People drink water and say—it is simply water; fire is simply fire. But even fire could be investigated from the point of view of the Fiery World. Beginning with the diversity of electrical manifestations, it is possible to arrive at the luminosity of objects and animals. One can find in certain species of fishes interesting degrees of luminosity. If we begin to analyze the composition of this luminosity, we can see, besides the ordinary processes, something indescribable, especially among deep water creatures. Amidst these compressed organisms appears one of the qualities of the subtlest Fire. Thus it is possible to observe comparable data upon antipodes. Amidst rarefactions of the air and amid ethereal explosions similar differentiations of Fohat are glowing. Beings

of the middle strata cannot endure the pressure of the oceanic depths, just as they are not adapted to ethereal vibrations; nevertheless certain hints may be found in observations which are already taking place. With sorrow did We follow two scientists—one descending into the depths, the other striving to the heights. Both had useful problems, but neither of them had in view the study of the degree of Fire, as an element. Naturally, their attempts were inadequate. Remarkable are the depths, and the heights still more so. But the basis of striving was right. Gradually there may be found apparatus sufficiently protective, but if the problem of spatial Fire will not be dealt with, again useful possibilities will be lost. In the fiery body we observe a great deal, but only with the help of Hierarchy. But it would be extremely opportune if scientists would put before themselves the problem of the Fire of space. Even by means of hints they would arrive at the realization of the pressure of the fiery element. Our disciples sustain it by the prophylaxis of the heart, but for the crowds, hints from various sources are needed. Crowds will perish from the fiery element. Why then do they not attempt to learn about this element?

129. I do not advise middle measures. To affirm the transitory state as a completion would be contrary to evolution. When a prayer is uttered about rest with the Saints, it reveals ignorance in regard both to rest and to the Saints. You know that rest is a purely temporary state, and in addition is relative. The so-called Saints have no rest. It may be said that the expression used is a relative one, but by respite people understand a state of repose. But if people were to be told about tension in the Fiery World, only a few would comprehend such an attribute of the higher condition. When We speak about a state of continuous explosion during

65

the highest tension, it does not strike the imagination to recognize such tension, so We say—not tension, but splendor! The path to such grandeur is through the beautiful. If man will not develop within himself an aspiration to the most beautiful, he will close his own eyes, but the Highest can neither be repeated nor imagined. The manifestation of splendor is absolutely infinite. Still, let us not hold open the middle measures of sleep and rest. I affirm that repose would not produce the manifested Universe.

130. Who will ask for an admission to a pit, as if wishing to pass through the entire thickness of the planet? The radiance of the Heavens must attract even him who is most perplexed in mind.

131. Let those who study the Teaching examine more frequently their understanding. Not only those who are just beginning, but all must pay attention to their consciousness. It is said that consciousness has a gravitation toward involution, but this merely means that the consciousness, as a most subtle substance, must be always nurtured.

132. The mightiest Avatars do not bear upon themselves signs of earthly distinction, but they affirm themselves by manifestations of spirit-creativeness. One should not be surprised at the fact that strong spirits may not be recognized by their contemporaries. Thus it should be, because their measures relate to the future. A code of laws may be made for only one portion of the approach to any successive step of life. Consider that people cannot ever recognize that the highest attainment is in the development of the heart. Cooperation and close living together are based upon the heart. It seems this simple truth cannot be realized. Mechanization impedes the basic penetrations into the Fiery World.

133. Certain metals are easily combined, but others repel each other. One should observe these lines of good and evil. Both sides create complete connected chains. But the chief impediment of government lies in the mechanical mixing of opposite principles; hence comes premature dissolution. Heart and Communion with Hierarchy will tell where would be the combinable parts. Man is in need of equilibrium of mind and heart. Cooperation is confirmation of equilibrium. The sacred number of Pythagoras is the equilibrium of Beauty. Much of this axiom has become inapplicable at the present time. It is a weighty task to speak to people about equilibrium.

134. Competition is one of the difficult concepts. Only the fiery heart understands how many measures may be placed upon the light and upon the dark side. A pure understanding of self-perfection will not evoke competition. Where the consciousness is wild and unrestricted, there competition leads to mutual destruction. Envy nests around competition. It leads to the most subtle crimes. Cooperation must bring balance to the misunderstood competition. It is not easy to fix for oneself the boundary of a reasonable competition. The word competition itself is already dangerous; in it is expressed jealousy, in other words, a corrupt devotion. Therefore, it is best wherever possible to replace the concept of competition with that of perfectionment. A great number of concepts must be revised from their contemporary connotation. It should be acknowledged that a just history of beliefs would reveal the roots of many most perverted concepts. Care should be taken that the language of the basic ideas be resounding and as clear-cut as possible. One may enrich the language with new definitions, but senseless buzzing will not bring any benefit. Each letter denotes by its sound a vibration of the centers. It is foolish to infringe uselessly upon harmony. Turn your attention to the resonance of the ancient names of places. The new places do not always produce the same useful vibration. The ancient names had a timeless significance. Often no philology can discover the root inserted by manifest powerful peoples. The more carefully, then, must we regard an inheritance which is unknown but which forces our hearts to resound.

135. One may recall a fairy tale—A thinker brought some people a wonderful curative remedy, but it was necessary to carry it in a closed casket. None of the people would consent to open this casket, because, judging by their own natures, they assumed that it was a viper or some kind of poison. Thus one may offer a most beautiful treasure, but people will take it to be poison. This is how people impelled by fears of misfortune accept a treasure. What, then, is to be done if Satan has so firmly implanted distrust.

136. Blessings to those who even once have reflected over the fact that possibilities are being given them for Service. One such thought already opens the initial Gates to the Fiery World. Whoever thinks in his pride—"Only I myself will attain," makes use of possibilities of serving his own ego. What an isolation resounds in boasting to oneself! What solitude is the prison of egoism! But it is joyful to think—"Yet I can bring to Thee, Lord!" There are no limits to such heart offerings! Is not the heart being exalted in trying to find the treasure of the offerings? The subtlest thoughts surround such supplications. Of course, the offering of the heart is really a prayer. It opens many gates. Not the consciousness of one's merits, but the offering of oneself in all entirety, helps one to pass over the threshold. When the gift is complete it leads past all frightening manifestations. One may say to the dwellers on the thresholds—"I've no time to gaze at you!" Thus, the offering brings ease.

137. Actually it is inadmissible to try to alter Karma willfully or forcibly. The Lords of Karma add each violence to the chalice of condemnation, but They can lighten Karma where perfectionment and offerings are without end. Thus do we lighten the paths to the Fiery World, when we are willing to do the best possible. It is not for us to measure what is best, but the heart's desire leads to the radiance of the gates. Restrain each thought about self, but permit the heart to lead along the shortest path. The heart has been given as the focal magnet to the Fiery World. Not without reason do many hearts grieve, both on the Earth and in the Subtle World. Of course the nature of the heart is fiery, and it sorrows at all obstacles which prevent its return to its native land.

138. It is correct to refrain from spiritualism. The dark ones have chosen this path for the penetration and sowings of evil. It is possible to think with purity about everything, but a clouded consciousness finds in everything the path to obscuration. Especially at present it is necessary to avoid any obscure channels. One must go toward the Light with all striving. I assure you that it is necessary now to be strengthened in heart, for the time is full of poison.

139. Who will keep silent when blasphemies are uttered? Each living heart says, "We are not with you, blasphemers!" The disease of blasphemy is very dangerous. But no justification is to be found in the fact that this is a disease, as this ailment is very disgraceful. When the heart is alive it will oppose in every way the infection of blasphemy. One can call to mind heroic

oppositions even on the part of children, when their hearts were pure.

Be blessed, you who take a stand against blasphemy!

140. It is necessary not only to recognize that there is no void, but also to understand the surrounding life. The understanding of life as intertwined and mutually nourishing brings realization of the omnipresence of psychic energy. On the very smallest examples, in incomplete micro-organisms, one may study that which is strikingly all-saturating. Varied currents, rays, and chemisms pass through masses of beings, but psychic energy not only does not retard them, but transmits them farther. When we speak of the most pure air, even about the purest Prana, we nevertheless presuppose all-containment, and in this containment various tensions. Picturing such physical saturation will aid the realization of Higher Worlds. Actually, everything is alive, and everything manifests the same energy. In this primitive position rests also the possibility of transmutation of everything existing. Death becomes a transposition and life becomes unavoidable cooperation. The very approach to the Fiery World is application of conformable qualities. It is sad to see how people limit themselves and try to harm the universe. Perhaps overproduction, competition, and distortion of the meaning of life will bring humanity into a blind alley, and then it will be obliged to stop and think. Because, by setting aside all limitations the recognition of the Higher Worlds will come along. Calling to the Fiery World, we must have recourse to comparison with micro-organisms, and thus impel people to think about a saturation with uninterrupted life. Indeed it is easier to think with the heart, above all microorganisms. It is necessary to summon to such a solution.

141. It may be observed how furiously people are now objecting to the concept of Leader, and at the same time they are ardently awaiting him. It is instructive to observe the disunity of the processes of brain and heart. The brain follows the conventional thinking and repeats sing-song formulas. But the heart, even though it be weak and unbalanced, preserves grains of Truth. Where the brain finds strength in negation, the heart, though timid, still is atremor with joy at the nearness of the manifestation of a solution. People who raise objections against a constructive move usually have nothing to propose in its stead. Indeed, such objectors are among the first to follow a Leader. They will whisper about disagreement, but willingly and precisely will they carry out a Command. Not because of their slavish nature will they accept Hierarchy, but due to the labor of their hearts. This means that in a moment of danger it is necessary to maintain equilibrium around a strong authority. Therefore let the Leader not be confused by these phantom voices.

142. Why so many tests, if the heart can create spiritual transformation? The answer is simple—the heart has been neglected and not applied to life. Thus many people must improve their consciousnesses in trial. When you hire servants, you either test them by designating a task, or you trust them after looking into their eyes. Thus, too, the heart can flash out convincingly in a glance. But reason may compare the eyes to pewter cups. Thus, at each possibility, advise the way of the radiance of the eyes.

143. What is love of good? It must be understood that it not only includes the performance of good deeds, but also the ability to be enraptured by good. The latter condition is usually not assimilated, and remains misunderstood; it must be inculcated and cultivated in people. Only delight in good produces warmth of the heart. The manifestation of love of good reveals a multitude of details of good which are touching in their essence. Many useful comparisons may be overlooked which can refine the heart. Such refining will guard against inflicting of an offense. Each offender has already closed the Fiery Gates; he has made an attempt against human dignity, and thus, first of all, has belittled himself. When I spoke about the Fiery World, then love and good was naturally to be understood as a firm foundation for ascent. And how beautiful it is to be able to rejoice at good! How exquisite it is to be able to distinguish the petals of the Lotus of Good! And We rejoice at each manifestation of such joy. Surely such joy about Good is pure! Thus, let each one who dreams about the Fiery World first of all supply himself with love of good.

So tense are the times, that I will issue an Indication—Let each offender blame himself, as We will not protect him. There are enough complications. We must justly measure out energy. Let each one ask his own heart—Where is the boundary of offense? It is inadmissible to misuse forces in mutual injuries.

144. Conformity of the qualities of consciousness creates the possibility of entry into the Fiery World. Thus, side by side with love of good must be aversion to evil. Love of good alone, without aversion to evil, will not be real. Aversion to evil is a highly active quality, it is the touchstone against evil. The mind cannot sufficiently well discern evil. A great many reasonings may be found in which a viper is concealed. But the heart feeling of repulsion to evil does not err. The nerve centers revolt against contact with the dark principle. It is impossible not to notice this heart sign, and then is created the resistance to evil. One may observe how the heart current immediately strengthens the armor of radiation. One may say to such a warrior—Verily, brother, you have armed yourself. Or, as one hermit compared himself to a dog sensing a wild beast—Though the eye see not, nor the ear hear, yet the heart has already sensed and armed itself, for evil is not endurable for the pure heart. Evil can adorn itself with many garments, but no mask will deceive a vigilant heart. So let us study the qualities needed for the Fiery World.

145. Sometimes you see yourself in an exact replica, as if alive before you. Such a vision demonstrates that the eye is only an accommodation, and that sight is in the nerve center. Such a tension of the center can be also regarded as a fiery quality. In the Fiery World there is vision of the spirit, which is not in need of ocular adaptations. It is easier to become possessor of the fiery eye if already in the earthly state one has been able to have flashes of such spiritual insight.

146. Fulfillment of wishes takes place much more often than is thought. But one must acknowledge such fulfillment. One must perceive the very beginning of such movement. There are many cases when people rudely cut short the beginnings of the fulfillment of the desire. Also in this regard one may advise to avoid irritation and doubt. As clouds conceal the sun, so does irritation sever the conduit of the heart.

147. In any object there are to be found side by side perfect parts and chaotic particles. It is possible to call to action either the perfect or the chaotic portions of each thing. Outside of magic invocations, against which We have spoken more than once, every man, by means of heart energy, performs continual evocations. When a man thinks about the inconvenience of an object it actually becomes inconvenient. When a man thinks about a beautiful object its perfect particles begin to act. Ignorant people attribute such a manifestation to auto-suggestion, but those who know the nature of things understand this as magnetism of thought. Of course, it is manifested in various degrees, but always it can be observed that the object is, as it were, animated through human thought. Man has but to realize this natural force to apply it beneficially in all the circumstances of life. Thus, known Yogis often advise their disciples to talk to objects. Words are ships of thought. Thus, as long as we do not learn how to deal with objects, we shall not grasp the power of thought for the Fiery World. Consider it fortunate that also in the earthly thought it is possible to become accustomed to the proper treatment of objects.

Is it not beautiful that even the most ungifted people can summon the beautiful particles, and can arrest the flow of the chaotic ones? It may be understood that our senses also become sharpened upon recognition of life in everything existing, the life in which we participate.

148. Mementos easily take on the significance of talismans. Also memorial days affirm a useful rhythm. It may be understood that mementos awaken tides of love, and bring a purification of the aura.

149. Forgetful about everything, man forgets his own destiny. Not without foundation is the legend mentioning the animal state. Many examples have been given to man in order to warn him in good time, but never before have there been so many animal-like people. And the external covering merely reveals the inner ulcer. The Teaching calls upon people to help themselves and to respect their own nature. But the deepest, darkest ulcer is considered fitting for those who trust Satan. It is difficult to imagine how many people are addicted to Satanic rituals! Entire schools are busy spreading such harmful principles. Much already has been told to you about terrors, but when I see new transgressions, I cannot but warn you once more. Be not surprised at dizziness and headaches; each particle of your energy is tensed and on guard, for it is necessary to protect you from many projectiles. Unprecedented necromancy is being applied by the dark ones, in order to summon the very lowest spirits; for they are indifferent to consequences, they wish to be strengthened for just one hour. But a counter-blow is naturally drawing near.

150. One must distinguish precisely with whom one can work, but if a choice of co-workers has been made one should not remind them about the past. Who knows what may have happened in the past! Usually people are obscured in the snares of the past. Indeed, it completely prevents one's being turned wholly toward the future. And what small earthly stones of the past prevent one's proceeding rapidly on the path! But one should become accustomed to the hurried path, no other exists. A great number of unfortunates and sufferers are counting the moments, waiting for help. Indeed, ought we not hasten?

151. One should strictly distinguish between a contradiction and a particular manner of work. If a left-handed person can create with the left hand, the significance of his attainment will not be contradictory to right-handed work. But people are hampered by the conventionalities of measures; even at present they cannot comprehend wherein lies the value of labor, and each unusual method immediately arouses suspicion. What a nasty quality is suspiciousness; it has nothing in common with the Fiery World! The approach of suspiciousness makes man worse than an animal, for the latter retains his instincts whereas suspicion corrodes all the senses. Indeed, it is a survival from the darkest past. Fortunately it is subject to cure by suggestion, but one should not neglect such an infection.

152. One must grow to love the path of the Fiery World. No striving is of assistance if it is not protected by love. Precisely the fire of love, in its chemism, is closest of all to the Fiery World. Thus, even in difficult days let us generate the currents of love. Rarely do people understand that love is actually a fiery principle. Usually people suppress the most salutary qualities of love. Precisely by these qualities does man most easily overcome the manifestations of darkness. Let us not cite examples, but merely emphasize the healing power of love. People especially respond to healing power. They dream about the elixir of life, but beyond a life on Earth their poor imagination can suggest nothing. Thus, let us not forget that imagination is a quality of the Fiery World.

153. It is possible to note not only a temporary absentation but also other related manifestations. For example, a man goes to sleep with a definite thought and awakens with its continuation on the next word. This means that his spirit has been absent on a completely different plane, and then again has joined his earthly consciousness to the definite word. This means that in the Subtle World a completely different plane of consciousness is used. Thus it must be. But when people preserve also there the earthly consciousness, then such clumsy thinking will be even harmful.

Imagine a man coming out of a dark and stifling room into a beautiful garden. If such a sharp change does not renew his thinking, he shows himself to be highly insensitive. Such personalities are to be found among soulless people. But how incongruous are they amid beautiful, uplifting surroundings, just like a filthy blot! But even earthly filth is not easy to remove; therefore We are anxious to project the consciousness through the Subtle World into the Fiery. Often such striving is not in accord with one's forces, yet even at worst it advances one in the spheres of the Subtle World. However, shopkeepers overcharge a great deal so that they may receive at least something. Not a great consolation! In order to advance somewhat in the Subtle World, let the consciousness be drawn into a most Beautiful Garden. This is Our Command—without small measures.

154. You have read that for communion with Higher Forces the ancients covered the head with a mantle, and, as told, this fabric was of wool and red in color. Also you may have heard about the stopping of the ears with red cotton. All such mechanical means had their significance, they served as a guard for radiations, and they condensed energy. But let us not resort to the expedient of mechanistic methods where there lies the utmost significance for the future, in the direct union with Hierarchy. Only the heart, covered with nothing but love, links us with the Higher Forces. The fabric of love is a most sacred one.

155. Does a man know when he performs his best action? What person can tell which of his words has had the most influence? What person can tell which of his thoughts has reached the highest spheres? No one knows this about himself. Perhaps such knowledge would cut short the striving for development, for it might stir up pride. Thought sometimes actually reaches the Higher Spheres, and, as a dew-drop, remains near the Altar. But one's own evaluation of such thought by earthly measure is impossible. People too often dismiss in disdain those thoughts which bring joy to the Highest Hearts. Thus, let us send out the best thoughts into the space. We need not adorn ourselves by the consciousness of our flights. Let them, as everyday nourishment, strengthen the heart for the perception of the Fiery World.

156. What is hypochondria? Many confuse it with auto-suggestion, but the latter is only an effect of the former. Hypochondria in its essence is very infectious and destructive. It can be defined physiologically as the dissolution of heart energy. Such a process interrupts the protective work of the nerve centers. The enemy's entrance into the stronghold is not a matter of auto-suggestion, but far worse; the defenders of the stronghold, instead of resisting, open the gates to the enemy. It is difficult to cure, for hypochondria is not always subject to suggestion. The process of dissolution cannot be replaced by suggestion. It is necessary to heal the wounded nerve tissue. Here strength can be built up only by nerve exercise. Consequently, hypochondriac people must be subjected to the most drastic influences, and to the most unexpected ones, in order to produce spontaneous tension of the nerve tissue. Such tension is like gymnastics for the nerve centers. Rest and disuse of the nerve centers is not always beneficial, notwithstanding the usual counsel of ordinary physicians. On the contrary, the ancient wisdom says, "You are afraid, therefore you will be doubly frightened." "You have ceased being afraid, consequently you can behold the Fiery Gates." Hypochondria must not be confused with doubt. True, these two are sisters, whose mother is ignorance. Hypochondria is a certain established mode of thinking, whereas doubt is a dark obstacle. It is difficult to say which of the vipers is the more harmful. One should free oneself from hypochondria as from an obstruction before the Fiery World. Many things are erroneously thought to be synonymous. Ponder over them, over different facets of definition. Who knows which of these will open the broadest vista in realization of cause and effect?

157. Certainly, cruelty must be eradicated; not only cruelty of actions but also cruelty of thoughts. The latter is worse than any action. It is imperative that the State take measures to prevent the inceptions of cruelty in infancy. Humanity must be purified of this most inhuman, dull and malicious darkness of low thinking, as of leprosy. Children are not cruel until they see the first cruel action, which reveals the current of dark chaos. Only a few are prepared to oppose the current of darkness. Such accumulation of consciousness is rare. One cannot presuppose such attainment in everyone; on the contrary, one should take measures befitting a lower step. Likewise, let us not repeat in a moribund manner the great Commandment, "Thou shalt not kill!" But let us ponder where is the greater killing, in the hand, in the word, or in the thought? One should reflect that the thought of people is ever ready for murder.

158. You yourself know that the most sure path is the path of altruism. Let us recall the dangers we have escaped through magnanimity. Perhaps we do not even know the limits and dimensions of such dangers. But the heart bears testimony that precisely good-will did help in the most difficult hours.

159. Correct is the comparison of the quality of the substance of thoughts to that of gases. Each gas, besides its already disclosed qualities, has many others which do not lend themselves to investigation by physical apparatus. No one dares to affirm that the effect of a gas has already disappeared, it can only be said that our apparatus no longer registers the effects of the gases. But to what extent a gas transmutes the space into which it penetrates, and how much influence it has on human beings, no one can say. Likewise, the limits of the field of expansion of thought absolutely cannot be defined. Similarly, no one can determine physically to what extent thought can influence life. It is amazing how the life of strongly hated persons sometimes is not subject, as it were, to danger. There are many reasons for this. Perhaps this person is needed for the Karma of an entire country. Perhaps the thought is not strong, and unrhythmic. And finally, perhaps the accumulation of thought will begin to act not immediately, but tomorrow. Earthly measures are in this case also relative. Especially is the thought weakened by the lack of understanding of Karma. Many efforts are needed in order for man to keep in mind the beautiful law of cause and effect. One advice may be given—nowhere to yield to the counsels of malice.

160. One may apprehend through many examples how wisely are distributed the Hierarchic forces of advancement. You yourselves see how a Worker, revered by you, remained in the Ashram because His spiritual forces were ablaze near the hearth of accumulations. Only the ignorant think that from earthly considerations alone He did not come out into the field of battle. Everyone who has any conception of spiritual forces will agree that only their conscious application will be wise. Thus, let us realize goal-fitness; it is needed immeasurably on the path to the Fiery World.

161. Reverence of the Teacher is a remedy against all ailments. When very ill, turn to the Lord.

162. You find it difficult to translate the phrase— "he became completely imbued with." You are right, in languages far removed from Sanskrit it is not easy to find certain definitions, particularly relating to the Higher World. One may have to express it as—"he became aflame" or even "he took fire," in order not to abase the concept of exaltation. Many misunderstandings are included among the definitives. Expressions which are striving on high suffer especially; only people who so strive themselves can use them, but there are not many of these. Therefore languages begin to rotate around petty concepts; they improve in mechanical expressions, but it is not even considered necessary to find the consonance of Higher Worlds. Turn your attention to newly coined words. Through them is it not possible to estimate the level of consciousness! But one should also honor the Higher Worlds with exquisite expressions, so that the Fiery World could also be glorified in earthly sound. Thus let us reiterate, in order that youth may find time to advance the thinking upward. From the quality of the thinking is born the word.

163. One should not be distressed in carrying out the Indications of Hierarchy. Many fruits become bitter from vexation. In many things it is necessary to draw close to higher understanding. For example, one should conquer the feeling of distance. Certainly it does not exist for the spirit, and if we shift our consciousness into the spiritual sphere then our feeling also will shift correspondingly. In other words, it will become broadened. And in addition, communion with Hierarchy gives, as it were, a new musical key to all our actions. Thus let us be closer, still closer, so that no viper may creep in.

164. Observe how people are to be distinguished in thought and in action. People should be judged by their works, but it must be borne in mind that only conformity of thinking, word and action is of assistance at the approach to the Fiery World. One must penetrate thither through all the poisonous gases. So many consciousnesses must be brought together in order to avoid deviation from the path. Many voices will call and many forbiddings will resound, but one should not look back. One should know one direction, and know not to change the destined. Thus, let us apply the same law throughout life. Whoever thinks it possible to act differently is mistaken; both in the great and the small there is one law, one rhythm. Thus let us proceed, without vexation.

165. Vexation is the plague of the World. It reacts upon the liver, and engenders certain bacilli which spread in a highly contagious action. The Emperor Akbar, upon sensing vexation in someone, would summon musicians so that a new rhythm would break up the infection. This action, even though physical, brought beneficial results.

166. Upon pressing or rubbing of the eyes colors appear which act as crude reminders of the radiance of the centers. If a coarse contact can produce evident illumination, then contact of a higher energy can certainly bring beautiful colors of the spirit. From the gross to the very highest it is necessary to cognize the saturation with spatial Fire. One should become accustomed to conscious acceptance of spatial accessibility. However, one should adapt oneself to such a merging. Let us not forget that ancient revelations were given for the betterment of life, and for the refining of consciousness. Thus the bond with the Higher Worlds was maintained directly. But later, because of the breaking away, quests for mechanical methods began, for the purpose of preventing a complete severance of the communion. It should be borne in mind that during Kali-Yuga such methods became ineffectual, and even a mixing with the lower strata of the Subtle World took place. But Satya-Yuga, by its very nature, requires communion with the Higher Worlds. Therefore, in preparing for Satya-Yuga one should turn again to direct communion with the Higher Worlds, by applying true Ethics. This is needed for destined discoveries which cannot be given to an animal consciousness. I will not weary of reiterating it, for each hearth of enlightenment of the spirit is important. Where, then, can be the paths to the Fiery World, if not through the decrees of Ethics? Surely Hatha-Yoga does not lead to the Fiery World. Enough of preparations—one should hurriedly strive toward the Higher Worlds. Let each of our cells contain millions of millions of currents. Not for somnolence have the subtlest apparatuses been given. Not for the sake of doubt are there being made calculations involving such huge figures. They surely remind one about Infinity and the saturation of all that exists. Thus let us be imbued with thoughts about spatial Fire, about the possibilities of our being. Satya-Yuga cannot draw near without fiery signs.

Along with the approach of Satya-Yuga let us not forget that the destruction surpasses measures of equilibrium. People do not suspect to what an extent the earthly currents already have been violated! They do not wish to understand that this cosmic disturbance is taking place through their own fault.

They consider themselves teachers of knowledge, yet the simple law of good is not convincing to them.

167. Examine two stones. They are primitive, cold, they have become congealed in their small life, but even they can give off sparks of fire. The heart of a man is no worse than a stone. The thought of a man, even in a small manifestation, is higher in effect than a mineral. I speak of this because it is instructive to observe how thought evokes sparks of fire from the innermost memory. The most casual thought evokes whole forms from the storehouse of memory, entire epochs in which we have been participants. This is a procession of definitely related fiery contents. Indeed, the spark can extricate related portions from the preserved treasures with instantaneous speed. One may be amazed how securely the treasures lie in the Chalice always ready to be drawn out. Only fiery energy can act so subtly and swiftly. The fiery earthly manifestations give an idea of the tension of the Fiery World. If here on Earth something can be astonishing in its speed and accuracy, then how keen and swift is the Fiery World! If only people would not forget about the Fiery World, one link could be established. Think what the state of consciousness must be, when one is obliged again to remind about foundations which are so near. However, let us reiterate, let us be filled with patience. It has been said—affirmation of Truth is a strengthening of the bridge.

168. In general, food is not needed in the usual quantity. It is wisely said that eating is the chains of the devil. Many generations have been burdened by gluttony, therefore caution is required in applying counter-measures. In the final analysis, more people perish from over-eating than from hunger. But a gradual process is required always in overcoming atavism. It is impossible to abolish over-eating all at once, but it can be pointed out that all superfluous food is harmful.

169. The cry of the heart is generally understood as an abstract concept, but Ur. says not so, for she has known and heard the resounding of the heart in its great tension. Such sounding actually occurs, and in it is expressed a powerful energy. The most dangerous assaults of darkness are shattered against this tension of energy. But not often is it possible to attain such a striking aspiratory state. The fiery heart knows when the invocation of the entire psychic energy will be demanded. From the solar plexus, from the chalice, there is concentrated a current of powerful force. The most evil sendings will fall apart under such a discharge. We always rejoice at seeing such a vigilant heart, since the attack is always sudden and the accumulation of force is only possible through great watchfulness. Often this keen vigilance becomes clouded by a kind of faintness which is very indicative of the presence of dark forces. But a flaming heart does not give in to such poisonous chemisms. But remember that evil forces do send double, repeated blows, knowing their effect upon unprepared organisms.

Strengthen your guard greatly after the first trial.

170. Many suppose that scientific data will shield them against cosmic manifestations. They will tell you about their knowledge of eclipses, they know about sun-spots, even about the appearance of comets, and hitherto unknown rays, but they cannot anticipate the appearance of meteors, which may be of gigantic dimensions. But if people know about the discoveries of huge fragments of spatial bodies, they can likewise imagine the possibility of devastating consequences from them, which should bring to mind the fiery bodies.

171. People complain that the picture of the Fiery World is not clear to them. Let us not insist as to who is at fault in this. Let us propose to them that they picture the Fiery World in their own imagination. Though such visualization be a poor and hazy one, let it begin at least in some way. It thus can be utilized as a beginning, but it is bad when there is nothing upon which to build. Such a state of indifference grows worse as time passes, and, as a stone, it drags to the bottom. No one can arbitrarily overstretch the boundaries of consciousness. The middle path is excellent when it is also lofty, but many cannot altogether understand the lofty concepts of the middle path, and confuse it with the path of vulgarity.

172. Due to unsteadiness of thought people see neither joy nor danger. But let us ask them always to ponder when the heart whispers about threats or about new joy. Likewise one should not be surprised that the dark forces can approach the most sacred places. But you have already seen such manifestations and know that absence of fear is the first condition to halt any evil whatsoever. But let us be honest with ourselves, in order to determine where there is fear and where it has been driven out. Fear is a weapon of the dark ones.

173. Let it not be thought possible to deny the Invisible. It has been said that there does not exist action which can produce no consequences, but this is particularly true of negations. One may often ask oneself—why is the evolution of the world so slow? Negation will prove to be one of the principal causes, for it is deadly. Like doubt, it cuts off all the ordained possibilities. People given to denial eventually have to live through its consequences. Truly, negation is like a millstone around one's neck. Enough has been said about it in the Teaching. But now, especially, the Earth is infected with negation. Let multitudes of people imagine that negation is only a sensible criticism, but negation is not a judgment, it is like ashes banking a grate fire. It suppresses, but does not elevate. Only broadening of consciousness can shame the denier, but as a rule such a torpid state terminates in a grave illness. In many cases a physician should attentively converse with his patient prior to treatment, in order

to ascertain his mode of thinking. Each illness from negation reveals the need of suggestion in order to arrest the destructive process. Some may ridicule the fact that for the treatment of cancer and tuberculosis it is necessary to begin with suggestion. Of course, physicians who do not possess the power of suggestion will protest in every way, and they will be highly provoked upon hearing that diseases of the liver, stomach, kidneys, the gums, and rheumatism depend largely upon the state of consciousness and require suggestion first of all. It therefore follows that it is necessary to regard suggestion and auto-suggestion seriously. Both processes are of a fiery significance. Thus negation is in opposition to the Fiery World.

174. Not infrequently do children manifest the better thinking about the Fiery World. Try to encourage them in such thinking, while applying subtle understanding, for otherwise one may either turn them away or else impose upon them one's own personal conception. Let children draw from their own treasure-house; it is ever ready to reveal the most vital details. Science can obtain valuable data from children; too little use is made of them. And people abuse children, being unwilling to understand how much can be harmed by a rude touch.

175. The young generation too often leans toward coarseness. Such a situation is highly deplorable, when tension of all the best forces is required. It is most necessary to reiterate that any coarseness is unsuitable for evolution. When there are so many cosmic dangers men must understand that coarseness is ignorance.

176. Amid observations upon the deplorable consequences of negation, one should not blame certain well-intentioned people for applying their own force first rather than trouble Hierarchy. It may seem at

times that people act from self-confidence, when, as a matter of fact, they are filled with reverence for Hierarchy, and above all they strive to apply their own forces in order to conserve every ounce of Higher energy. They do not even pronounce the name of the Teacher, and they guard their mantram in secret. One should regard very carefully the various modes of reverence. One should affirm all that aspires to the Light. With Us only negation is rejected. Indeed, the very existence of man, who thinks and who contains the subtlest apparatuses, is a real miracle, which could not be without a past, and hence not without a future. The Fiery World is the predestined future. Who, then, will hesitate on the path, knowing the great destination? Who, then, will not respect the present incarnation, knowing that it will aid the ascent? Who, then, will disdain the Subtle World, knowing that there is the testing of thoughts? Thus, our brief sojourn here has been bestowed as the best aid toward a speedy advance to the Fiery World. In some way one should combine the urgent problems of life with the highest resolutions. Actually the earthly life hinders speedy realizations. People dream about the mechanical prolonging of life here, instead of cultivating a joyful readiness to approach the goal. The Teacher brings the consciousness of the disciple, by the shortest path, toward the attainment of the Fiery World. The Teacher affirms all that which may, even indirectly, bring closer or unify useful consciousnesses, in order that each action contain within itself the necessary amount of conditions of approach.

177. During the crossing into the Subtle World there flash out all the aspects of the feeling of possession, which troubles even people who are not at all bad. One should assiduously keep in mind this circumstance, and be affirmed upon the realization

that earthly possession does not exist. A great deal has been said about personal possession, but only the fiery state can prove the illusion of such sense of possession. Only when our consciousness remains our sole possession do we feel the freedom of ascent. It is very difficult to balance the ascent which goes beyond the middle strata of the Subtle World. Therein people do not even think of parting with various kinds of property; indeed, they exist just by means of these attractions. But if a higher manifestation raises their consciousness a bit, there begins an incredible conflict. Therefore, here in the earthly state one must apprehend where lies the useless burden. This should be done not in the name of the Subtle World but in the name of the one higher.

178. Some may wonder why the signs from the Subtle World are so strange and why they require pondering and interpretation. The reason for this is the law of Karma. Precisely reflection and explication stimulate self-activity, and, thus, they lighten and even do not produce Karma. Consequently, the stronger the attentiveness and resourcefulness, the more easily interpreted are the given signs. The Lofty Beings do wish to give hints toward a great many things, but the mental distraction of people prevents these precious Counsels from reaching them. Not only in sendings from the Subtle World but also in earthly existence, parables have been adopted, as a means of indirect indication. But history sets forth many instances of non-acceptance of the most urgent counsels. Not without reason was attentiveness so developed in antiquity; it even constituted a study in itself. But nowadays not many understand the significance of vigilance; for others guidance is required in the sharpest, and repeated, instructions, which cannot but have an effect on Karma. But only the fiery heart will comprehend the hidden meaning of subtle signs. Let the co-workers grasp the fact that each sign has its destination. So many Lofty Beings send supplications and hope that they will be understood. There have been whole epochs when the subtle understanding was strengthened and sharpened, but later a bloody mist condensed anew, and the refined perceptions became coarse. Just now many attempts from the best strata of the Subtle World are being rendered futile by the dark forces.

179. I entrust you to testify about the Fiery World as existing, with all the attributes of existence. Fiery blossoms are distinguished by their radiance, but they may be compared in structure with roses; small vortical rings form, as it were, a combination of petals. Similarly, ozone, in the higher state, reproduces, as it were, the odor of evergreens. Also, the radiance of auras is like cloud arches, and rays are as streams and waterfalls. Thus, in the higher forms the wise one will find likenesses of earthly images. He will not see the earthly existence as abased thereby, for in all states of being the foundation of energy is the same. The wise one will not seek a precise counterpart of God in an earthly body, for only the fiery body will preserve the same sparks as the Higher Beings. Should it not be pointed out in schools wherein we are like God, so as to justify the ancient Teachings of which people have made a laughing stock? Everywhere the highest concept must be clarified. One must not fear to come forward and help wherever it is possible to elevate the consciousness. The Teaching is in need of those who will bear witness. It responds to all, without distinction as to creed and nationality. Above all let the one sun shine. It is not difficult to speak about unity, through the path of science. Let the manifestation of beautiful correlations unite the most diverse elements.

180. Do not confuse fatigue with intensity. These two states, notwithstanding their complete difference, can produce similar symptoms. But fatigue must be overcome by a change of work, whereas tension must be actually increased. It would be a mistake to allow oneself to dissipate tension. One must nourish this manifest fiery power as a precious gift. Each tension is a sharpening of consciousness. Each weariness is a dulling, but in either case let us not forget to take musk. Ur. has wisely established the combination of musk with soda and valerian. Certainly the very speedy accumulation of musk by means of soda is useful, as it is also the continuation of the use of valerian. All three ingredients are of a fiery nature. Not without reason was soda called, in antiquity, ashes of divine Fire, and fields of soda deposits were called sites of Devas' encampments. Likewise valerian is especially effective in combination with musk. While musk kindles Fire, valerian sustains it as a static condition. In fatigue this fiery remedy is absorbed in order to renew the nerve centers; but in the striving of intensity there is need of prolonged combustion, in order to avoid explosions and shocks. But above all other life-giving agents is the communion with Hierarchy. Musk may dry up, but in communion with Hierarchy its strength will be promptly renewed and an inexhaustible supply of energy extended.

181. New circles of disciples must be attracted through the heart. We regard as an attainment not only the direct transmission of the Teaching, but also the indirect saturation of space with It. The Teaching should not be pushed there where there are no doors.

182. Can the body be wounded? As on Earth so

also in Heaven. Consequently, the fiery body can be wounded, just as the earthly one. Observe the process of wounding of the earthly body, and you will have a complete analogy with the subtle and fiery bodies. Let us see how a knife pierces the physical body, how it damages tissue and blood-circulation; then follow local necrosis and decomposition; but vital energy gets the upper hand, and slow healing begins. But often there remains a local atrophy and a permanent scar. Precisely the same process takes place in the case of the fiery body, but instead of a knife will be a thought, and in place of a scar will be a condensation of fiery energy. But the healing is very slow, and requires the drawing of energy from the other centers. Each organism has a fiery body, and until it attains the Fiery World, it is subject to being wounded. Only when the fiery body has been purified and poured into the furnace of spatial fire, will it no longer be susceptible to being wounded. But I assure you, scars remain for a long time. I affirm that the fiery body can be smitten both externally and internally. Suicide of the earthly body is the prototype of self-wounding of the fiery body. Thus is it possible to find of the most earthly actions a correlation in all states.

183. Much has been said about life in the Subtle World. The accounts often appear to be contradictory, but again let us take earthly examples. The diversity of earthly situations is astonishing, only undeveloped eyes are unable to distinguish great numbers of subtlest manifestations. When We speak about earthly situations, We usually have in mind only uniform groups, but We cannot enumerate the entire complex of volitional creativeness. Therefore Our definitions will depend upon the theme of the discourse, or upon the quality of the consciousness of Our listener. Likewise among the truest descriptions of the Subtle World there will always be found groups, corresponding most closely to Our designs. Thus, let us not criticize the diversified aspects of information about the Subtle World. If the earthly world is stately, then the Higher Worlds are progressively majestic and multiform.

184. Circular motion is in everything. Vortical rings are not only in the strictly physical world, but also in all thought-forms. One may observe how the circle of each task is culminated. We have already advised alternating work for the renewal of strength. Such manvantaras may be observed even in the smallest tasks, but they will have the same significance as world manvantaras. Thus, outside of circles of daily labor, one may see the manifestation of the circle also in entire periods of activity. Precisely the fiery heart will whisper when such a ring is complete, in order that a new manifestation may be taken up. One should not overload a consummation, yet it is still worse to complete a circle artificially by violence upon life. Thus, one can study in history how cycles of activity are moulded. The fiery principle is expressed in such vortical rings. One must be prepared for such construction in the Fiery World also. It should not be thought that the Fiery World is an already perfected condition. Systems of Worlds, of which we see only a negligible part, present an inexhaustible variety of conditions. From here we cannot analyze these states, but it is useful to dream about them. Each dream is already a realization.

185. Calamity has actually arrived. People ask—Wherein is God's wrath? It is in such calamities as people's turning away from God, their becoming traitors, either in actions, or in thoughts, or in the silence of fear. Let us not enumerate all the aspects of such treachery; it infects the planet and manifests an unmistakable quality. Humanity should not be surprised at ensuing calamities. Let man reflect—has he always acted in purity of attitude toward God? Has he always abstained from blasphemy, and was he able to keep himself free from evil thoughts? Thus people cannot say that the might of God is not manifested. He does not punish, but He can turn away, and then gold will be turned into a consuming fire.

Then will equilibrium be transformed into chaos, and the power of Earth may be exhausted.

Much blasphemy is everywhere. Derision of the Divine Principle is frightful! People have ceased thinking, and even their going into temples is often no better than a violation of them.

186. Fiery sparks also illumine animals. In this, one may observe a remarkable law. Animals receive fiery sparks particularly through contact with man. Likewise does man nourish his own fiery body through communion with Hierarchy. One's consciousness must accept the realization of the logic of Jacob's ladder; all creatures can find access to it when they are imbued with right striving.

Thought about good is blessed. There has never been a thought about good which has not produced the best fruit. But gathering of fruit requires practice and labor. Sometimes the reaping is even more wearisome than the sowing.

187. As has been said, the Subtle World is now also undergoing a great conflict, which is even more terrible than the earthly one. It may be understood that defeat in the Subtle World is inadmissible. Such a defeat would break through a chain of worlds, and would be highly desirable for Satan. Therefore the

Teaching so emphasizes the heart in order, at least a little, to prepare the people for cooperation.

188. The nature of things must be taught among the most primary subjects. It must be beautifully described in all reality; the succession of worlds must be demonstrated with all scientific comparisons. Not only will religion not contradict such exposition of the foundations, but on the contrary religion will assist, through its most ancient allusions. The study of the nature of things will serve as the threshold to understanding of Living Ethics. One must realize why honor, dignity and all other high human qualities are indispensable. From the earliest years children should hear about the Subtle and Fiery Worlds; they must understand the principle of Hierarchy and of Good. The sooner they are reminded about Hierarchy and the other Truths, the more easily will they recall former knowledge. The concept of God in all its grandeur is clarified on the basis of Hierarchy. Only thus can the Highest Concept emerge from abstraction and blend with all Existence.

It is necessary that the Leader and the Government understand how to increase the realization of the Higher Representation. It is necessary that schools attractively depict Existence in all its grandeur.

189. Among fiery signs there is the particular aptitude for finding needed objects. One has but to think about them, and they draw near, as it were, and are discovered. Already in antiquity it was said—kindle the torch of the heart and find that which is needed. The symbol is true enough, for the fire of the heart kindles surrounding fires and creates a magnetic attraction. Also in books, what is sought can be found by illuminating the book with the same fire. The more such a quality is observed, the more it is developed. The fiery element loves to be noticed.

190. Danger is a concentration of the vibrations of tension. A great number of perils surround people, but only a few of them are noticed. When the Leader says, "live in danger," he might well say instead, "observe the dangers and thus succeed." One cannot live outside of dangers, but it is beautiful to make out of dangers a carpet of achievement. The Leader knows that he bears a mission, and dangers are only propelling forces; therefore the Leader does not even think about dangers. The very thought of peril is harmful. Thinking about dangers, we strengthen their vibrations, and thus disturb our equilibrium. Conservation of forces must not be disrupted by fear and confusion. We are watchful and careful for the best execution of the commission. But dangers cannot overburden our attention. The Teacher should, first of all, insist upon the disciple's liberation from the phantom of perils. The disciple should always remember not to expend a drop of the higher energy uselessly. Thought of danger agitates many of our centers and in disorderly fashion consumes the precious energy. Thought of danger reflects even upon the pulse; but the heart is strengthened by the desire to carry out well the mission. Thus, let us act in the most efficient manner.

191. On entrance into the monastic life all difficulties of such a path were usually pointed out. Some would say—all is easy; others would warn—all is difficult. To people with fiery heart one may say—all is easy; but for the ordinary consciousness it is better to caution—all is difficult. If someone takes to flight at a single warning about difficulties, then he, all else being equal, is unfit for persistent labor. One should not gather together people who are obviously unfit. Fear of labor is already a treason.

192. The Alexandrian philosophers used to say— Do not criticize the World, for it was created by great thought. The creation is not at fault, but our conception of it is. We can channel our thoughts either for good or for evil. We could transform the best animal into an evil creature. Cruelty on one side and fear on the other fills our consciousness by means of thought. We can send evil in our glance. We could turn a beneficial plant into a most poisonous and pernicious one. The thoughts of the ancient philosophers penetrated into religions. Clement of Alexandria knew how people themselves debase the great Creation. Even now people may observe how evil can transform the most harmless beings. Indeed, every animal tamer can tell how often precisely the element of good assists him in his work. But he also knows that besides good there must be measures for self-protection, varying according to the character of the animal. Such a science may be called goalfitting. We cannot criticize the World without wondering why malice was allowed to enter it. So too, protective measures will emanate not from evil but from good. Each leader may be advised not to forget the advice of the ancient philosophers.

193. You already know sufficiently about the temperance of certain characters. What is to be done when moderateness has crept into the broadest circles? Those who are seemingly the champions of good give themselves up spiritually to moderation. One can see that the dark ones do not often suffer from this defect. There is a story about a devil encountering an Angel. The Angel said, "Thy servants are bitter." But the devil replied, "Mine are bitter, Thine are sour; we both must look for sweet ones." And the Angel was crestfallen for He could not prove that they had not turned sour. Thus was it observed long ago by people.

194. You will have to repeat to many that Our remedies are good, as a supplement to psychic energy. Some physical remedies cannot produce the desired result, but psychic energy is reinforced by communion with Hierarchy. Thus, the wise physician first of all will take care to know the condition of his psychic energy and to see that it is in concordance with the Higher Forces. Paying attention only to physical qualities has no significance for the future. When We speak about the Fiery World, it means that it is time to be moving forward. It is impossible to remain on the level of the transitory period, when all the foundations of Existence have been forgotten. I affirm that each physician must pay attention to himself in order to feel to what an extent he himself is ready to renew his consciousness, otherwise he will not find fitting words for those who come to him. He will be unable to inquire into the actual causes of ailments. He will not maintain a self-affirmed influence. I do not insist that each physician be a hypnotist, but he must understand the spiritual world of the patient in order to be able to speak about the main thing in the case. The Teaching must disclose paths, but not be merely a pharmacy. Let people have an opportunity to observe and discover, otherwise there will be reactions upon Karma.

195. A new tradition about the significance of the heart must be molded when people are caring least of all about it. Institutions for the study of the heart must be founded, with a knowledge of all that has been written about this center of being. All the ancient cults in which a place was allotted to the knowledge of the heart, must be studied; and here external remedies alone are of no assistance. Let us not forget that in antiquity suggestion was applied for reanimation of the stopped heart. There are many traditions about the bringing back to life which are based on this action. True, a great and disciplined will is required, and time is needed for the establishing of the new heart action. It must be determined how many minutes must elapse before the heart activity can be again established. But this will be extremely variable, for the actual departure of the subtle body occurs quite individually. There are many reasons for this, including the physical state and the quality of the subtle body. The physician should understand this diversity of conditions.

196. The bodily movements of man must be intelligent. Children must be taught not only gymnastics and rhythm, but also the meaning of economy of movement. When people apprehend the Fiery World and radiations, they will not senselessly wave their arms and legs about, shake their heads, and be fidgety. If they could picture to themselves their auric egg, they would not disturb it needlessly with disorderly agitations. If people could picture a sort of fiery ring which is in reality around them, they would not senselessly burn themselves. Especially unjustifiable are so-called nervous movements. They indicate an entirely undisciplined will. Each physician must observe such habits of his patients. It is possible to determine many diseases by a man's movements alone. It is possible to cure him of the most disgusting habits by observing these movements and pointing out the harm they do the subtle body. Thus, a physician can manifest a most useful activity without physical medicine.

197. Who said that musk is merely a stimulant? It can have an equilibrating importance, bringing into motion basic energies. It is regrettable when such multiform, powerful reactions are reduced to a single manifestation. The poorer the idea of it, the cruder the hypothesis. This refers also to many indicated remedies. No one thinks about the significance in synthesis of valerian. No one is willing to understand mint as a friend of life, ready to exercise a calming effect upon rebellious centers. No one wishes to observe the action of milk combined with soda. Thus broad is the field of observation for eyes which have been opened.

Mint can be useful even as an indoor plant, for the emanations of its living leaves are most subtle and natural, as are those of roses. Where one can have flowers, oils are not needed. Thus, the most alive and the most natural are the best of all. Let us not forget that mint and roses are excellent disinfectants.

198. The Fiery World requires, first of all, the discrimination between small truths and Great Truth. Nothing else turns people aside from the paths to the extent that a little truth does. They snatch out small fragments, not thinking about that which precedes and follows. Such fragments are no better than any lie, but the significance of the Fiery World rests upon the greatness of Truth. One must prepare for it by all measures; it is impossible to suppose that the understanding of the magnitude of Truth comes of itself. The consciousness must be prepared for a containment of such dimensions. This is not at all easy. One may see how erroneously the simplest words are understood. It is even difficult to imagine to what an extent the meaning of the most ordinary word can be distorted. But one should pass through the testing of so many diverse concepts. Only the acceptance of higher dimensions will evoke the Higher Call—Raj, Raj, Raj! The threefold containment can lead to the higher spheres. Raj does not know revenge and censure. Raj is magnanimous, because directed into the future. Raj wishes for good, for it is creative love. Such a measure guards against the small truth, which comes close to the evil, and to doubt and to condemnation. Thus, when you wish to temper the spirit, you can repeat the ancient Mantram—Raj, Raj, Raj!

199. When I remind you about the ancient Mantram, it means that a great truth must be revealed, and that one should act by great measures. One is not saved by words but by their application. Thus, there is no small truth in this, that already a great measure is required. And let the thought be a joyous one, that already Raj has been pronounced!

200. One can turn to good from any path of evil whatsoever. But such possibilities are most appreciable in view of the problem of progression. Actually, each lingering in evil carries one away from good in rapid progression. Thus, where yesterday it was possible to jump off the chariot of evil, it is already impossible to return to the same place today. Everyone must be reminded of this who thinks that it is equally possible at any time to cast off the burden of evil. Its substance is very sticky and is overgrown with small truths, of which We have spoken.

201. People who take upon themselves Great Service may be called "Heavenly Stones." In their striving they fill themselves with light. They pierce through the lower strata and contain within themselves diamond-adamant. But it is not easy to be a diamond, and it is necessary to be affirmed in light in order to conquer darkness. Great Service knows no repose; by incessant vigilance is the spirit strengthened. A heap made up of small earthly truths must be covered with the dome of magnanimity. One must be under the cover of Light issuing from Hierarchy, and must assimilate the Subtle and Fiery Worlds as in the nature of things. From a pit one may not notice the sun; yet people study the stars from a well. The most unexpected may happen on the path of Service, but the experienced Leader will not forget that each worldly loss is made up for in space.

202. Nowhere do people think about the Living Ethics. They think it possible to pass their lives in the usual way, yet with each day it becomes more evident that it is possible to save people only by means of faith, which surpasses all religions. There is not much of such faith, and let us not try to count in thousands where there are only tens. Unusual are such paths of realization of the Highest.

203. The three Worlds are far closer to each other than one may think. One can see how corresponding vibrations create cooperation. You know how certain individuals from the Subtle World who are close to Us act to assist a common task. Even not so long ago they were unable to serve the common purpose because of difference of vibrations, but now your vibrations and their endeavors for communion make them useful co-workers. Thus is created useful labor in common. It is the more useful because the adversaries have similar co-workers. Certainly, it is joyous to watch each cumulation of consciousness. Ur. has seen how in the beginning the atmosphere is dim and in the course of successive meetings it becomes lighter, and a day ago Ur. saw completely conscious cooperation. Such an enlightenment is very rapid, yet for this the Ashram is of significance. Verily, Ashrams have a great importance for the earthly and for the Subtle World. Ashrams may be defined as magnets and ozonators. Being filled with heart energy provides a conduit for many things. Therefore, when I am concerned about spiritually pure atmosphere, I have in mind a very important consequence. Without spiritual accumulations, the command to take everything upon oneself has no meaning. This command can be given only where there is a heart bond with the Subtle and Fiery Worlds. Only such a bond, during the present earthly conflict, can strengthen those to whom the order has been given. The currents are too complicated to be opposed by earthly forces. But you know about the bond with the two Worlds. Precisely in this communion are found forces for the passing by the most unexpected path. In this, do not hesitate to take care of yourself, in order not to expend energy superfluously. One should not in any manner be diverted from inner concentration. The affairs of the whole world are in a grave state.

204. It may be asked—How many times should the Teaching be read? Answer—It is impossible to set limits for that which one loves. One may know it by heart, yet one may nevertheless wish to read it over again. When we memorize it we establish a certain rhythm, yet a new reading may give new enlightenment. It will not only enhance the understanding, but the very change of light on the book may bring a new approach. Therefore when I say—Read the Teaching both morning and evening—I have in mind different circumstances of time. One thing will be noticed in the morning while a completely different one will be apprehended by the evening fires. Understand this literally. Evening thought is distinguishable from the thought of the morning. One should compare the two.

As thought at evening is broadened by the light of the lamps, so does morning thought glow from contact with the Subtle World. Morning thought is strong not only as a result of rest, but also from contact with subtle energies. But evening thought is distinguished by the complete exaltation which is akin to living fire. Many suppose that they already know the Teaching when they have read it through once. But the best precepts remain unapplied, because people are unwilling to understand their polychromy. Thus, examine the crystal of the Teaching by sun and by firelight.

205. The word chorus is used to mean a consonance of voices, but there can be a chorus of energies, a chorus of hearts, a chorus of fires. The Teaching must turn your attention to the choral principle, which does not interfere at all with the individual principle. One should develop within oneself cooperation, in order to bring about a direct increase of possibilities. Thus, care about the choral principle is linked with constructiveness. People can understand that a chorus needs all kinds of participants. Only very experienced leaders understand why there have been needed participants who are not very active, yet who can bring in originality and harmony. The Teacher rejoices at each originality, in it is born a new aspect of Fire.

206. Let us observe how nations can perceive the significance of knowledge. We exercise care that the manifestation of knowledge should proceed by an unusual path in order to strike human imagination. Actually it is not easy to know how to awaken the imagination of past incarnations; only a purified consciousness which is not confused by transition, manifests continuous imagination, ever new and untiring.

207. The greatest earthly cataclysms have resulted from under-sea ruptures. Let us not forget that while mountain peaks attain the height of **30,000** feet, submarine chasms even surpass this measure. They may be pictured as reaching a depth of **70,000** feet. The disappearances of lakes are not so dangerous, but a rising of the water level should be a matter of concern. Several times the Earth has undergone the same fate, but people do not think on a planetary scale. Just now there may be observed a certain resemblance to past events. The lack of balance of fires and waters constitutes a subject for deep investigation. Some will ponder over it, and many will ridicule.

208. Often the Teachings have warned not to judge the dead. Among the many reasons for this there is one which very closely concerns earthly actions. We have already spoken about co-workers from the Subtle World. It is difficult to judge from here as to who has already developed an aptitude for cooperation. It can be imagined how unjust it would be to censure such a co-worker, as condemnation naturally repels. There are many such assistants, and one should value them. When imagination has been developed, such cooperation can easily progress.

209. The picture of present-day reality is still more unattractive. One must value highly the periods of time during which there was no blasphemy. Has not this viper poisoned the present state of affairs? We are much troubled to see how senselessly people limit their lives, not thinking about the great miracle which each man bears within himself. To each one has this marvel been allotted. The purse of the heart is identical in all—place therein the treasure!

210. The spark of immortality is justly located by certain people in various centers, each will be right in his own way. True, in each center there is such a spark, but according to the conditions of the epoch the centers can vary in significance. Only the heart remains unchanged and only the chalice follows the heart in significance; the remaining centers and glands may be subject to cosmic currents. Not only are people mistaken in their judgment about the centers, but everywhere they do not admit a flexible expediency. Yet not only according to the epoch is the significance of psychic energy altered, but also according to races, to nationalities, and even to generations. Seemingly, a thing re-occurs, but meanwhile man has come in contact with the Highest by means of new antennae. Thus, one can observe how multiped insects may lose certain legs without a lessening of their vital capacity. Certainly where there is the fiery consciousness such atrophy of the centers is not found. Hence, again we come to the affirmation of the usefulness of the fiery consciousness. It will be no exaggeration when we say that fire is advantageous for the earthly as well as for the Fiery World.

It is asked—What center is particularly important just now? The present is a time of synthesis, therefore let us begin everything from the heart itself. Precisely the heart stands above all. Therefore, let the throat and the chalice and the solar plexus not be isolated from the guidance of the heart. The throat is an instrument of synthesis, but transmutation and its application take place in the heart.

211. You have already seen that thousands of people may perish in a single hurricane. Is it possible that the manifestation of ominous storms does not impel humanity to reflect as to whence comes such imbalance that not only hurricanes and earthquakes, but even floods reach the highest dimensions? It is a fact that millions of people have already perished. But the consciousness continues to grow worse. It would be fair to ask humanity how many tens of millions of victims are required before a change of consciousness is recognized.

212. Courage is required when in the atmosphere itself there is observed an unprecedented tension. One can sense, as it were, the presence of a certain heat, notwithstanding an outward freshness of weather.

Even the influence of cool currents does not free one from an immediate sensation of inner heat. One must notice how this internal heat is characteristic of atmospheric fiery tensions. Thus, not the shoulders, not the throat, not kundalini, but the heart absorbs the currents of external fire.

213. By all means one should assimilate the basic law that the Teacher gives the direction but does not fix the details. One must seek and find them in labor. Especially confused is the understanding of the greatness of the law of striving which directs to discovery. Not only now but even in better years people have always demanded complete formulas, although they do not think them out for themselves.

How instructive were the tests wherein from an initial letter a disciple had to find the whole required word. But not many will seek such a unified consciousness. It must be pointed out how much such searches reinforce the guidance. Not to a prepared meal does the Teacher summon one, but He knows places in the forest where one may gather ripe berries. To this place of blissful harvest the Guide summons, and He regrets if the disciple prefers to buy unclean berries in the market place. Thus does Guidance flow through the heart, when the solicitous Hand imperceptibly directs toward the best path.

214. It is necessary to learn not to require elucidations when I speak in symbols. If the language of the symbol was needed it means that just now the ordinary means of communication would be useless.

Then I say—Make a note of the symbol and keep it in memory, against the hour of its application. Likewise, observe the indication toward certain countries, which means that Our attention has been turned to them. Such guide-posts are of assistance on the path.

Thus, a frightful time is being filled with salutary fires, but Karma will not be overburdened. It is not good when the Guide has to press upon the Karma of the disciple. One must grow to love the salutary milestones which flash out in the heart at the approach of events.

215. One may speak and write about a symbol, but it does not follow that a teacher must translate the symbol into ordinary language. We do not come too late with warnings when they are necessary. Likewise the names of the countries will soon rise up before you and you will distinctly apprehend how We consider these events needful and instructive. But do not forget that Ur.'s heart is on a lofty fiery step and perceives very clearly. One may surmise that events are under pressure, if the heart and solar plexus of Ur. are so tense.

216. It was affirmed many times by the philosophers that a gathering of people is permissible only when it has a high moral consequence. Obviously this saying is a strange one for our time. A gathering of people now usually ends in distortion of the simplest precepts. Let us look upon the subtle and fiery surroundings of such populous assemblies. Let us look and be horrified: discordant rhythms admit only the lower entities, and transform the fiery sendings into searing fire. If it is difficult for an earthly benevolent visitor to make his way through a beastly crowd, then subtle beings will be flung away like dry leaves in a whirlwind.

One must await the time when during lessons in psychology counsels about mass reactions will be given. People are willing to join an organization, but they are averse to cultivation of their own will.

217. You have been writing today about physical remedies, but for crowds even barrels of the most

precious substance will be useless. One may urge all physicians of the World to start upon a mission of spiritualization of the heart. Each physician has access to different homes. He sees various generations, and his words are listened to with attention. When giving physical instructions he can so easily add the most valuable advices. He has the right to be acquainted with all the details of the moral conditions in the home. He can give advice which will compel the occupants to reflect over and above the actions of the stomach. He can even command, for behind him stands the fear of death. The physician is a most sacred person in the household where there is a sick person. And since humanity has taken care to collect a sufficient quantity of diseases, the physician can give many valuable warnings. If we but had enlightened physicians! At present there are so few! The more do We esteem enlightened physicians, since of course they are always under the threat of expulsion from the Medical Societies. Heroism is needed everywhere where the Truth is.

218. Ur. has seen and taken part in Our Fiery labor. Thus, We not only observe but also control fiery tensions. Centers of observation are situated in several floors of Our Tower. Many forces have been collected to oppose the fiery attack. Satan is very anxious to make an end of the Earth, in order to concentrate his forces on the Subtle World, which cannot be destroyed in the same way as Earth. Thus the Proprietor of Earth through present treachery is betraying the Earth. He is a poor Proprietor in that he cultivated such a nature within himself. He causes Us double labor by keeping up the fires of chaos. Ur. has seen not a few apparatus; but over and above them stands psychic energy, and therefore We are so careful with it just now.

219. Very often misunderstandings have occurred

as a result of relativity of definitions, which have undergone changes through passing centuries. The most ancient writings have undergone many alterations, passing through the hands of foreign translators. It is a well known fact, but for all that it is not taken enough into consideration. To obtain the full meaning one must turn to the same source, Hierarchy. If the translator and interpreter is in communion with Hierarchy, then his relative understanding will be set right in due time. It is unfitting to touch the Sacred Teachings with dirty hands. All forms of blasphemy are condemned, but it is especially abominable when a servant of religion blasphemes. Unfortunately such cases have become frequent. There are not a few actual atheists among the servants of religion. Is it possible for them to speak about the Living Ethics? The madmen do not wish even to think about the future life. One can imagine all the horrors of an assembly where blasphemers are gathered! The Fiery World is just a farce for them.

Let Our friends not hesitate to speak wherever possible about the Fiery World. Of course, besides the spiritual point of view there can also be a scientific approach. In addition let Our friends themselves think more often about the Fiery World; such thoughts are as prayers.

220. Fiery labor is indeed full of dangers. Ur. already knows how fiery tension acts. Not only in the earthly body but also in the subtle it is impossible to withstand for long such tension. Besides, We focus the vortex upon Ourselves, so that a discharged arrow will strike in a center of tension. This method of focusing is employed by Us everywhere. On it is also based the *Tactica Adversa*; from it flow the drops of perspiration, about which you know. But in all, centering is preferable to scattering.

The apparatus which were seen by Ur. are of enormous force; they are condensers of fiery tension. Thence comes the idea of the swastika. Scholars must review the ancient signs; in them will be found hints of many of Our apparatus.

In the case of such a special problem as that of Earth, chaos represents a great danger.

221. Threads of the spirit are spread far more widely than people think. I say repeatedly—write down, even if it be briefly, the sensations and the strivings of the spirit. From such writings it will be possible to make significant deductions. Likewise the physicians can make use of this valuable material. Possibly, not always can such writings be compared, as a great deal may not coincide so easily, but even isolated cases may assist someone to recognize the psychic energy. No special university courses are needed for this. Psychic energy especially acts freely, when man is aflame with hearty striving. The measuring rod of psychic energy is pure striving. Not magic, but pure human striving will produce a marvelous world.

222. Ur. has again taken part in fiery labor. To a perceptible extent the inner fire has also appeared externally. It is evident that each approach to the intensified energy burdens the physical organs. Only self-sacrificing spirits can render help. It must be understood that the extraordinary tension indicates agitation of the elements. One must rally all forces in order to preserve concordance with the Fiery Forces. Verily, there are many black stars. Each day only serves to complicate events.

223. Above all else I am concerned with the imbalance of the world. Obsession is developing, and it threatens to become insanity. Many countries are governed by madmen in the fullest meaning of the word. Never before has this manifestation of mass obsession occurred. Why scientists do not pay attention to such a calamity is incomprehensible! People commit millions of murders. Is it possible that no one realizes that this is a hotbed of obsession!

224. Investigate, and distinguish two kinds of thought. Everyone knows that at times, in the midst of clear thinking, there appear confused, floating thought-forms. Some will advise to ignore these unclear smudges of thinking, but others will recommend the investigations of such visitors. There can be advancement from paying attention to such thought-forms. They come from without, which is but the more reason why we must not cast them aside. Who knows—perhaps they are directed to us intentionally, and are not clear merely because of their dependence upon our attitude. Therefore it is best to take pains not to reject any thought, even a fleeting one. When our heart is aflame, it quickly senses the value of such sendings.

225. It is an error to think that irritation of the nose, throat, and lungs is caused only by colds. Such tensions also result from spacial fires. Without doubt, irritation of nose and throat can be cured by suggestion. The same cause underlies many cases of so-called hay-fever, which often can be cured by suggestion. Also many kinds of skin disease are cured by the same method. Often, in fact, skin irritations arise not from external causes but from imbalance of fiery currents. It is regrettable that physicians do not observe this phase of human ailment. Only occasionally do they recognize nervous causes, but then they try to flood them out with bromides, whereas suggestion could produce a better result. Let us not forget that at times suggestion has been employed to speed up the closing of wounds, by way of enlisting the cooperation of the entire organism. Thus, during discourse about the Fiery World, one should not forget the cause, at times, of irritations of the nose and throat. Physicians must be urged to study all methods of suggestion.

226. Dreams link us with the Subtle World, and in the same way there must be correlations also between the Subtle and Fiery Worlds. They exist in their own form, but not everywhere are such contacts with the Fiery World of a conscious nature. One must possess a developed consciousness in order that such samadhi be not blinding. Already on Earth one must prepare oneself for the fiery approach. Thought can make the conception of Fire perfectly natural. With the help of such simple and natural conception the approach will be affirmed without any difficulties.

227. One's mastery of thought does not consist alone in the deepening and concentration of thinking. One must also possess the knowledge of how to free oneself from untimely and debasing thoughts; thus thought is affirmed when we master it. It is not easy to free oneself from thoughts flying in from without, and it is difficult to cast off sad and burdensome meditations. But one should be able in like manner to send thought forward, and also to leave behind the one which is of no use. Usually, people are enslaved by their thoughts; and nothing so impedes advancement as grievous immobile thoughts. Most often such heavy thoughts are sent from without, and many eyes watch with malice, awaiting the suppression of energy. Learn to expel this obvious burden immediately, it is one of the worst aspects of Maya. Hardly a day will pass without an alteration in Maya. Thus, let us be doubly vigilant in possession of thought.

228. Usually people do not even notice the turning course of circumstances. Yesterday your attention was directed to the fact that people do not wish to understand that they themselves create! The ladder has long since been constructed, yet man nevertheless casts himself into emptiness, for he thinks about a former ladder. It seems impossible to affirm people upon reality. The simplest and most beautiful solutions are passed over in silence, and rejected merely upon the assumption that somewhere grandfather's ladder has been left standing. It has ceased to exist long since, but the average consciousness will not accept such reality.

Let the grandeur of the Fiery World advance people to the steps of reality!

229. A good attitude is still far from acceptance and excellent relations. One may recall an old fairy-tale: A grandfather prepared an unsinkable fabric for his grandson, before the latter put out to sea. But the grandson covered the roof with this cloth. Thus, when the storm struck, his ship and he quietly went to the bottom, and his grandfather was unable to help him.

A man often puts a saddle on a cow and later is amazed when others, on horseback, outrun him. One may but smile bitterly at useless expenditures.

230. Striving is regarded as of true value. No one of those who strive with the heart will be forgotten. Of chief importance is one's own consciousness of purity of aspiration, but there are not many who can confirm a purified striving. Thus it is possible to single out people according to their striving. The energy of pure striving is highly homogeneous, and the bearers of this energy actually constitute a universal body. They may be working in the most diverse fields, and nonetheless the essence of the kindled energy will be one. Therefore people are divided not according to physical specializations, but according to tension of striving. Know that difference in nationality has no significance; to the fiery substance neither race nor age can mean anything. Where the heart is aflame people seek communion and exchange, but they do not know on what basis to form contacts. Sometimes they are afraid of scorching one another, forgetting that identical energies are not mutually dangerous.

231. One should not be inordinately grieved perceiving human darkness. If We should exercise our grief in proportion to this darkness, it would be impossible to exist. It is sad to see how people impede their path, but the centuries teach one to assume calmness about the qualities of imperfection. Indeed, such qualities are especially deplorable when time is so short. But let us devote ourselves to Hierarchy.

232. Swelling and irritation of the glands indicates resistance to the dark forces. Obviously, irritation of the glands and of all the tissues gives aid like the help derived by the hedgehog from uplifted needles. One need not be astonished at such degrees of tension when each day is filled with madness.

233. The Leader is not dismayed by apparent failures, as he knows that the quantity of good can fill up any abyss. He will perceive any swerving from the path, yet it will but give him one more possibility to visit a new region. Likewise, in the hands of the Leader good becomes an actual manifestation of Light. The consolation does not lie in the fact that a failure is not possible, but in the fact that each achievement of good is a manifestation of new progress.

I do not advise you to count the signs of darkness, they lead only to obscurity. Light is one; Light can be a measuring scale and a support. The Fiery World was created by Light, and thought is a product of Fire.

234. It is not the brain substance that thinks. It is time to recognize the fact that thought is born in the fiery centers. Thought exists as something ponderable but invisible, and it must be understood that a lever is not a furnace. Already many truths are knocking for admission, but only thinking about the fiery centers can be of assistance toward correct interpretation.

235. One must observe how entire countries can be shaken by one incorrect interpretation. It is impossible to justify this by saying that someone did not know about something. Usually proof can be found that such knowledge had knocked at all doors, had lain on all tables, and had been mentioned many times. It is not right to try to justify inattention and unwillingness to think deeply.

New oppressions are nothing but unconvincing conduct of the Leader. Often people do not know the actual cause, but in their hearts they feel that something unconvincing is taking place. Most of all must a Leader guard himself against the growth of unconvincingness.

236. Let us affirm the enthusiasm of the spirit. To be filled with the spirit means to place oneself in direct communion with Hierarchy. All kinds of magical methods, even inner concentration, are used in attempts to achieve Higher Communion. But the new approach to the Highest directs one to the example of ascetics who above all approached direct Communion through the heart. We learn of prophets, saints, who never fell into a frenzy, yet their every word was the word from Above.

If you ask Me what methods are befitting our times, I say—you must prepare yourselves for direct

Communion. All conventional measures are already mediocre in themselves. In these days, when fiery energies have been so intensified, precisely this fire helps the heart to understand the Higher Command. This Command is propounded in the very midst of life. Then We say—harken and obey!

Each epoch has its expressions. One should not cling to old methods when it is possible to apply new understanding. Even in old Scriptures we see prophets who were always saturated with spirit. And much later, formulas, numbers, and rhythms were studied. But some have considered such methods too near to invocations, and thus belittling to the Higher Principle. Especially at present, during the epidemic of obsession, people must seek heart communion.

237. Deprivation of blessing was an act of the most ancient patriarchate. It is far removed from the later anathemas. Anathema is a product of ignorance, whereas the very ancient act foresaw rupture of the bond with Hierarchy. The bond with Hierarchy is an actual blessing with all its consequences. The ignorant will say, "We have many times defamed the Highest, and nevertheless we still exist; no fire has seared us, and nothing threatens us." Then let us lead them to the public square, where blind beggars are crawling in filth, and say to them, "There also are you." Let us lead them into prisons, into mines, to fires, to executions, and say, "Can it be that you do not recognize yourselves? You have just severed the thread with the Highest, and you have hurled yourselves into the abyss." It is not necessary to terrify with threats, life is full of examples of such horrors. Remember that the pressure of fire is invisible, yet nothing can escape its consequences. Thus, it can be seen that even the ancients understood the justice of the law, and knew that offense against the Primary Principles is so great and terrible that the result cannot be immediately seen.

238. The Fiery Sun is invisible, likewise invisible are great heavenly bodies. It should be explained in schools how insignificantly small is our field of vision. Only thus is it possible to convince humanity that while it is divine in its heart essence, in the body it is subject to all limitations. Only thus will children realize what they must be concerned about. They are very perplexed at that which is manifested in the chest and continually beats.

239. It is possible to perceive that even a small dark entity can concentrate around itself many powerful co-workers. One should not neglect any opportunity to evict dark hotbeds.

240. The consciousness directed to Us is continually being refined. The process of refinement becomes a code of every day. Could it be admissible that the subtlest energy be turned into chaos? Everywhere it has been said, "Whoever comes unto Me shall also abide in Me." This must be understood literally. The subtlest energy cannot be turned into amorphousness; therefore I am so concerned about refinement of consciousness. Complication by grossness only demonstrates that the heart energy has not reached a level where it is no longer threatened with drowning in the waves of chaos. One must hasten with the refining process. Each ulcer begins with the smallest decomposition of tissue. A drop of resin can make healthy the ailing tissue, but for a neglected ulcer not even a pot of resin can be of help. Create a manifestation of refinement in the very midst of life. Why only in words, or in glances, when heart energy is multiplied precisely in thoughts. The collecting of the most precious is only for the purpose of returning it. Who, indeed, would not wish to give something of the best quality? Only a cheat will try to offer something unfit or useless. One must keep watch over one's thoughts, in order to send those of the best quality. I am not speaking in the abstract.

Through you We send thoughts of magnanimity, and already much that is not good has been averted. Thus is a mountain of magnanimity molded, with a summit from which one can see afar. One may advise many of the panacea of magnanimity. We shall not tire repeating about this remedy of spirit and body. Some day physicians too will prescribe magnanimity as a most powerful antidote. Let us not forget that malice attracts the action of poisons, whereas magnanimity opposes them.

241. That which you direct toward Me grows as a thriving garden. The fruit ripens, but one should not admit worms.

242. One should not be surprised when We pronounce a name and thereby fill space with information. We affirm Our decisions in space. He who has understood the bond with Hierarchy must also assimilate the fact that the decision of the World depends upon filling the space. Truly, not the earthly world alone decides, but all three worlds. Thus, even apparently most positive earthly rulings are destroyed, because they have not been accepted by the two Higher Worlds. Likewise the dark forces must be sometimes informed, and because of this their wails merely augment the sound of the announcement.

Through all worlds is such a call resounded, and it stirs up new energies. Naturally, those to whom such a manifestation refers must be careful, for a vortex has been directed around them.

243. The principal danger lies in an incredible divergence of consciousness. While some almost

touch atomic energy, others have not yet reached even the cave-man stage of existence. Such a difference produces agitation of currents and makes movement difficult. It is possibly easier to move troglodytes than such heterogeneous crowds. That is why forward motion and broadening of consciousness have become so complicated.

244. Not only is the odor of the deodar pleasant, but it helps to invigorate breathing and expel dark entities. Many oils have a purifying property, but not all have an influence on the Subtle World. The deodar has a significance in the Subtle World, and it is usually connected with places of sojourn of the Rishi. They know that the deodar possesses the quality of driving away evil entities.

245. Our assistance is extended in the essential directions. It would be erroneous to think that the most petty details could attract Our energy. True, We always safeguard, but it would be absurd to think that every sneeze occurs by Our command. One must distinguish where are the most essential currents of life; only thus is it possible to learn to respect the fundamentals of Communion. Precisely likewise do We regard the Highest Ones. Evaluation of and respect for the energy will be a sign of understanding of Infinity. Reflect upon this deeply, as precisely at present fiery labor requires understanding of Our fundamentals. Is it sensible to turn away one's weapon before the blow is struck? Is it possible to turn aside the directed telescope without spoiling the observation? So too, when We bring cooperation near, especial solicitude is needed. Observe how I gradually deepen the conditions of Our joint labor. No repetition is ill-advised. We require what is reasonable to be required. Gradually We enter into dangerous spheres, and only thus may one expect victory.

246. The scholar is almost right in attributing life to the chemism of an organism, but he loses sight of the crystal of psychic energy. True, this most subtle substance is also a chemism of its own kind, but the approach to it is a special one. Usually scholars, among many true conclusions, miss the principal one, not so much because of opposition as from inability to imagine such concepts. You yourselves have seen two physicians to whom there was offered the greatest opportunity for unrepeatable observations. You saw how unable they were to appreciate these possibilities, and that they obviously evaded the chief consideration, while babbling absurd formulas. Cooperation lies in mutual solicitude and hearty labor.

247. Those uninformed in Great Service may even complain of the difficulty of such an achievement. But those in contact with it already cannot conceive of existence without it. A frightful emptiness appears, it seems, when there is no application of one's forces for Common Good. Without Communion with Hierarchy a terrible darkness closes in from all sides. Without Great Service, life itself, like a wilting blossom, loses its meaning. The Fiery World is intangible, and the very concept of it, instead of being attractive, appears menacing. Equilibrium is established by great measures, but affirmation of the Shield of Hierarchy comes after the dedication of oneself to Great Service. The spirit decides its own fate. Without any stipulations the spirit itself determines its sacrifice. The dimension of the sacrifice is decided in the heart. No one can force an enlargement of the offering, but much joy is felt from a sacrifice which is not diminished. The Teacher advises to recognize one's potentialities according to the sacrifice voluntarily accepted by the heart. How great is the law of such good-will! It determines the future, from small to big, and up to great events!

248. Reading without the heart's functioning, even memorizing, helps but little. One can even compile a table showing how much the participation of the heart evokes true understanding. Let this not be understood as an abstraction. By its quality the pulse indicates how much heart participation assists the manifestation of perception. Such a concept draws one near to the Fiery World. It is tedious to listen to babblings which lack the heart quality, particularly since the number of printed books is reaching frightening proportions. Rarely has the quantity been so at variance with the quality! In this is also revealed a sign of heartlessness. We encourage each burning of the spirit. The flaming heart is a torch of the Fiery World. One should become accustomed to delving into the meaning of what has been said; and for this, translations into different languages are useful. Thereby is developed a precision of understanding. The Teacher must always rotate a concept so that it contacts the consciousness of the disciple in its full scope. Though urgent, it is impossible to accept many concepts at the first reading. One must return to them, as has been said, under all the shades of color of morning and evening. Even the night will bring a ray of understanding. You yourselves have seen how strangely people form opinions about what they have read. When they hear about the Messiah, they merely think—isn't he a demon? When they read about the heart, they are afraid—isn't it sorcery? This means that demons and sorcery are very familiar to them. The man who is pure in heart will not think first of all about darkness.

249. Not magic but God-inspiredness was ordained

in the ancient Teachings. When Higher Communion began to be interrupted, people themselves compiled magic from the earthly world, as a means of forced communion. But, as everything which is forced, magic ends up in the darkest manifestations. The very boundary line between black and white magic becomes elusive in its intricacy. Therefore, on the path to the future one should eschew all magic. It must not be forgotten that the old methods of magic were connected with other forms of life. Of course, magic is based on precise fulfillment of technical conditions, but if all the formulas of life have been altered, then too all magical effects must be correspondingly changed. This is why contemporary magic has sunk into necromancy and the other low manifestations. All those who study the mechanics of formulas fail to take into account the fact that they were written down for a completely different application. In addition, they completely forget that the higher formulas, and all the conditions, have not been written down altogether; and if they have been noted at all it is in such symbols that now their meaning is quite obscured. Thus, contemporary studies of magic either amount to senseless scholastics, or else, flowing down, they lapse into the black mass. Therefore We speak much-needed words, in advising the abolition of magic. Let it be left to the dark necromancers. There is too much obsession on Earth. The sole path to the Higher Communion is through the heart. Violence must not stain this fiery path. Can people possibly think that the invocation of lower entities can go unpunished! And what sort of improvement of life could result from such evocation? No one can point to a benefit resulting from necromancy, nor to a heart which has been uplifted through necromancy. One must turn to the short and higher Path, which will bestow health of spirit; and thence comes the bodily health. The abolition of magic will be a white stone on the path of the World.

250. Despair is first of all ignorance. I am speaking not for encouragement, but for advancement. Many beautiful structures have been destroyed through unfitting despondency. It always attacks a man on the eve of complete attainment, when it seems as if someone has temporarily extinguished the fires; but the disciple does not know such terror.

251. The expulsion of magic does not mean interruption of the manifestations of the Subtle World. On the contrary, the bond with the Higher World can be but strengthened through the abolition of all violence. Precisely, ignorant compulsion can violate the harmony of combinations. Nature, both in the small and the great, is opposed to any violence. To study and to cognize the marvelous approaches to the Subtle World and to the Fiery World will not be magic. Prayer of the heart is not magic. Aspiration of the spirit towards Light is not magic. One must guard against all forms of ignorance, for it is a source of falsehood, and falsehood is the entrance-way to darkness. Be able to find in your heart the truth of turning to the one Light. Terror fills the world. Do not follow the pathway of terror. One may be fortified by examples of former times. The saints themselves were in contact with the Fiery World through the heart; the same heart which has been given to everyone. Ability to hear the voice of the heart already leads to truth.

252. A folk saying is a light in the window. There have been no untrue proverbs. Precious are the precipitations of wisdom. But just now there is before you a greatly confused time. One must summon all courage and find the right word for everybody. Manifested is the time of the awakening of the peoples.

253. Only the experienced heart apprehends the Maya of not only despair but rapture. It is not easy to show that rapture and exultation are not far removed from despair in their chemism. Exultation without a foundation does not resemble the wise joy when the whole heart vibrates with the Cosmos. In general, most people cannot endure residence on the Earth in continuous tension. Yet it is possible to inure them to conditions in certain chemical laboratories, where the newcomer is completely unable to breathe and where those who work there regularly do not even notice the pressure. Such an example must convince one of how possible it is to accustom oneself to constant vigilance, as to a magnet of tension. Whoever places foot upon the ladder of ascent finds the initial step difficult. Thus Maya passes into conscious realization of the cosmic tension.

254. It is a fact that there are many who would like to destroy each useful beginning. It is difficult to say who are the more harmful, the dark ones or the fanatics. Often the heart of the latter is even more inaccessible. Appropriating the inheritance of others, they have shouted the most merciless threats to all humanity. Be not surprised that they seize the best symbols and distort them. Not without reason have fanatics been called mutilators. One of their distinctive qualities is the lack of a sense of beauty. They can blacken the most beautiful thing, not through malice but from lack of a sense of beauty. Indeed, such failings go to make up a very dark stratum, but there are many fanatics, and they make difficult the path of knowledge.

255. It is understood that the stone-mason is required only to put stones together, but if he can save a man, must he refrain from doing it? Certainly there are not only stones in the World, there are also hearts!

256. Prayers often contain the supplications, "Look Thou upon me" or "Turn Thy gaze to me." In such words there is expressed great knowledge of the significance of the look. Precisely a look can change even the composition of the aura. Not only thought, but the very chemism of a glance has a fiery consequence. Those who know this ask the Higher Forces to look upon them, because in this magnetic chemism there is contained all-encompassing benevolence. Let us not forget that each look of a man has correspondingly the same significance; the more saturated with thought, the more powerful the glance. This is not direct suggestion, it is better to call it a saturation of space, for such chemism is disseminated far more extensively than may be supposed. The significance of the gaze can be shown when radiations will be photographed. One will be able to observe then the influence of senseless glances and of mental sendings. It is a joy to see how comforting looks can make the aura healthful. And such constant action can bring an enormous amelioration of all existence. Let us not forget that the presence of certain persons brings a considerable improvement in the aura of an entire assembly. They may be called Beacons of Salvation. Even when they are not directing energy their Od nevertheless penetrates the whole surroundings. Such natural agents of good health must be highly valued.

257. Each ejection of sorcery is a good deed. The more so since the danger from such action is great. One must have not only courage but also readiness of spirit, in order to understand how to proceed in each case. First of all, one must destroy the magic circle. But such contact requires a still more fiery tension than was employed by the conjurer. The discernment of the conformity of forces is achieved by straight-knowledge. It is impossible to touch the strongest flame without being burned; but when fiery energy gains the ascendancy there will be no terrible effects.

258. You may have heard that wise people, in an hour of danger, have sometimes exclaimed—joy, joy! This exclamation could not have signified mere self-delusion. They knew about the treasure of joy and, as it were, wished to draw therefrom a kindling of feelings necessary for achievement. Ghosts are not needed there where exists a sacred link with Hierarchy. One can borrow out of the Treasury inexhaustible forces, but they should be evoked flamingly. No one can oppose the joy of achievement. One should not submit to violence, but joy is a consummation. Thus, let us cultivate it as one would most precious blossoms, but let us not belittle it with the suspicion that it is an illusion. No, we know how joy resounds through the channel of Kundalini. We cannot often explain in words whence arises this joy, as a forerunner, but it comes to visit us on a light-winged ray of Hierarchy. Who knows from what Infinite Source sounds the call to joy? How many know that already the time of manifestation of joy has approached? But the law is immutable, and therefore joy is a special wisdom. How long ago this was said! But in spiral evolvement it gradually becomes real and comprehensible. Likewise grows the heart, and the consciousness, and fiery wisdom. We do not see how the grass grows, but we perceive the evidence of the growth. So too with the joy of achievement.

259. You have already heard about certain empty tombs. You have heard about a very ancient custom, when sometimes a substitution was made for one thought to be dead. It must not be forgotten that through the ages a great many extraordinary actions have been accomplished, and not just once had a life to be interrupted. People have been initiated into the mysteries of existence, and so many names have been inscribed upon empty sepulchres! Thus, apart from the beaten paths of history, inscrutable achievements are created. One must become accustomed in one's consciousness to a great deal which is not governed by earthly laws. Who can affirm how events are being created? One can observe only a few outward signs, but the real channel of life is not written down in the state archives. Thus, people are astonished when one who, according to a tomb inscription, is supposed to be deceased, re-appears ten years later and is identified by many persons. Of course, it is easy to overlook indisputable proofs. But honest observers can gather authentic evidence of many such events. Actually there is a history of the outer world and of the inner. It is not sorcery nor magic, but the path of the Higher World.

260. Become accustomed to My Advice that events are created by special measures. One should not weaken constructiveness by considerations of ordinary joy or sorrow.

261. It is an error to think that the forces of darkness attack only weak spots. Very often chaos presses deliberately upon the most powerful strongholds. Likewise breakers are more violent against cliffs. Therefore every wall must be guarded, both low and high ones. Let us not forget this, for people often think about shielding the weak and abandon the strong. Everywhere there are intimidations by chaos, and tensions are tripled. Read about the downfall of great nations to anyone who does not cherish the feeling of protection.

262. Yes, yes, yes, if people do not turn to the Hiero-inspiration, many conflagrations will result.

Equilibrium and concordance are violated by the mechanistic concept of the world. Half a century ago We were already concerned about the excessive increase of physical knowledge. Verily, much has been attained in this direction, but at the same time the spiritual consciousness was lagging behind the physical. Ethics were lost amidst accumulations of formulas. Machines attracted man away from the art of thinking. Now they are content to be robots! For the equilibrium of the World the heart is needed, and in this Decree is contained undeferrable salvation. Ill-will is pressing upon the earthly aura.

263. An experienced householder finds a use for all discards. The contemporary builder must undertake this achievement. It is an especially hard one, for it is not easy to make use of robots when the basic requirement is cognizance of the foundation.

264. Many do not apprehend that the Yogi must be extremely cautious in regard to his health. Through ignorance, many imagine that the health of a Yogi is assured, and that nothing physical can affect it adversely. In the opinion of some he feels neither cold nor heat. Whereas, an abutment of a bridge is far more assailed by the waves than is a swamp. The sand of the marsh does not undergo as much from the movement of the water as does the pier standing firm against the current. Therefore, it is absurd to suppose that the Yogi can remain unaffected by overburdening caused by ignorance. True, he will not make manifest his own tension, but it will be just as strong as is the fire of his heart. The simple law of correlation appears here also in full force. If some one should ask whether resistance is not developed against the pressure, the implication will not be devoid of truth. The more so must we maintain our strength, when we know for what it is needed.

265. Let us strive to understand the distinction of the most necessary. The determination of the degree of necessity is a quality of the Leader. One should know how to make a mosaic of successive order out of many simultaneous considerations. Neither logic, nor reason, nor formulas, but the fire of the heart lights the path of such a train of actions. One should realize with full heart where the passage-way is adequate, so as not to jostle a neighbor. The heart will indicate when not to overdo as regards pressure. Such testings of strength are known as the wings of justice.

266. There is no such thing as emptiness; yet often people sense, as it were, a semblance of emptiness. What can such an anxious sensation mean? Of course, it is not without foundation. With their thinking people poison their surroundings and transform them into chaos. The so-called feeling of emptiness is really a sensing of chaos. In itself chaos is not emptiness at all, but it is so far removed from the human consciousness that its approach already constitutes a loss of the guiding principle. Such a deadly principle is sensed as emptiness, and in it is contained no small danger; equilibrium is disturbed, and suicides and various kinds of insanity occur. Not emptiness nor chaos, but mean thinking causes the stupid poisoning of the atmosphere. Besides, such thinkers infect their surroundings and thus strike at their neighbors. Truly, man can become social only on a certain level of thinking.

267. Be not distressed if the Teaching be attributed to the most diverse sources, even to a code of most unknown writers. Perhaps it will be attributed to you yourselves, and such a circumstance will be one of the better ones. One should not even gainsay these inventors. There has never been unanimity in the world. Let what is of primary importance be accomplished. Let indications necessary for the betterment of life permeate the masses. Likewise be not distressed by individual opinion. When the name of the Brotherhood should not be spoken, let each one accept according to his consciousness. Indeed, the means of communication of information are beyond the understanding of people. But everything is done as is necessary.

268. It is very deplorable that people harm themselves by constant discontent, also the harmful disturbance of equilibrium extends into distant space. One can observe people, rational enough, nevertheless complaining of fate. Even earthly riches do not help them to banish discontent. Certainly, in general people do not usually think about spiritual riches.

269. The singular expression which you observed on the portraits pertains to the domain of Hiero-inspiration. Already in remote antiquity this spiritual penetration was understood. In ancient Egypt portrait images were used as a means of communion at a distance. Sacred Images likewise respond to spiritual communion. But this natural manifestation should be understood simply, as one more grain of knowledge, and not as magic or sorcery. No one can draft a boundary line to limit the knowledge of the spirit. No one has such an imagination as to be able to realize where the magnitude of energy could be cut short. Hence, one should conscientiously note all the understood details of various manifestations. One must rejoice at all such realizations, because these fiery beacons lead to the Fiery World. Consequently, on such paths one should apply great vigilance. One must accept reality as it is. Not distrust nor sleepiness, but the good eye and the opened heart lead to understanding of the new manifestations of the Fiery World. Observe how much the expression of the image becomes changed, and in the course of time you can compare this with events. It is needful, of course, to carry out observations upon people who have for you a special significance, and whom you know. The manifestation of such alterations of expression was called by the Egyptians the mirror of the soul.

270. Who can say where begins the Ineffable? Who dares to measure off somewhere something which is not permitted to be uttered? But the heart knows and can guard against a pronouncement of blasphemy. One must know how to hearken to such a sign from the heart. One must persistently and patiently cognize the signs of the heart. One must know how to turn to Hierarchy. One must realize that there is no other path. It has been said—let us devote our spirit to the Lord, but it was not said—let us overburden the Lord.

271. Sparks of Fohat indicate the degree of tension; there is obviously an unprecedented tension throughout the World. You do not know and cannot imagine the extent of the rencounters.

272. You have seen rings which changed their color, depending upon the condition of the wearer and upon surrounding circumstances. One could see that this changing coloration did not depend upon the quality of the metal itself. This means that an external chemism was precipitated upon the ring; but even so, such a phenomenon could not have been produced without fiery energy. Naturally, when it became possible to transfer this external reaction to the heart, the ancient phenomenon became unnecessary. It could be demonstrated, as mentioned in the most ancient literature, but energy need not be expended where the heart has already entered upon the fiery path of Hiero-inspiration. So too, in all the other manifestations

of energy, one must immediately turn to Higher Communion as soon as the conditions of the organism permit. The task of the Teacher consists first of all in the speediest elevation to the degree of Hiero-inspiration.

273. It can be seen how fiery energy surpasses all other energies. I consider that no physical energy can be manifested without an antecedent fiery impulse. Therefore each approach to the Fiery World is already a desired and difficult enlistment.

274. Excessive emaciation and corpulence are equally harmful for ascent. They equally nullify psychic energy. The middle path foresees the best conditions. Also, instead of a natural striving people prefer unsuitable extremes. The creativeness of the Cosmos does not tolerate lack of balance. It is known that chaos yields before the assault of the forces of equilibrium, but the same law must be introduced into all of life. We are microcosms and must be subject to all the conditions of the Macrocosm. But few people will even speak about such a condition of existence. Therefore such non-correlation agitates the Earth.

We have often forewarned about the possibility of a fiery epidemic. It has already begun. Of course physicians have not noticed it, for it appears in different aspects. The change in many symptoms of illness does not arrest their attention. Human judgment is too much attached to illusory forms which someone has accidentally observed. To alter their horizon is most difficult, but one should remind people that it is necessary to fulfill obligations. Often We send thoughts of magnanimity there where previously they were not even dreamt of. But even such unexpected good remedy is of timely assistance.

275. One may be astonished at the extent to which people attract only malice even from inoffensive

philosophies. The lowness of the consciousness which can only imbibe filth is amazing. Have people forgotten that every philosophy first of all forbids malice?

276. The very highest is Hiero-inspiration; it accompanies throughout life. No rituals are needed where there is the flame of Communion. One should guard the hearth of Fire. Even the ancients understood the symbol of the incessancy of Fire. Life must be filled with burning. At first man thought about himself, then about others, but afterwards his actions became useful for all that exists. He does not think any more about the usefulness, but he breathes it and gives life in Boundless Space.

277. Not only santonin, but also certain other vegetable substances help toward seeing the symptoms of the aura. However such mechanical reaction is undesirable. Each poison cannot but react on the nerve centers, if applied for long. When we come to speak about the fiery heart, this recognition of radiations comes about naturally. Besides, it is most fitting to sense the quality of the aura. Because many tints appear highly intermingled, and just the viewing of it does not give an understanding of their essence. Thus, sometimes a blue aura may be exposed to an undesirable yellow radiation, and as a result there is a greenish light, but such a combination can be distinguished from a pure green synthesis. Similarly, violet may be the result of the approach of crimson. Thus, a single glimpse alone means little. One must perceive through the heart the essence of what is taking place. Thus, for example, it may happen that due to illness the radiation will grow dim, but the fiery consciousness will apprehend that the nature of the radiation is not bad, and that only because of accidental sickness has it been temporarily changed. Likewise it may happen that the radiation may be subjected to an external influence, such as results from obsession. Here also only the fiery consciousness will apprehend the true cause. Therefore, when I speak about future photographing of the auras, it must not be forgotten that fiery straight-knowledge will also be needed for this.

278. The Teaching must first of all help the manifestation of justice. It must be foreseen that there will be cases when the details of the evidence must be observed in the light of fiery reality. There are many cases where from remote examples it is possible to judge about external influences.

279. It is possible to purify considerably the consciousness just by burning deodar. Likewise, Morua stands on guard and does not admit many undesirable visitors.

280. Esteem people who not only speak but also act. Affirm the ability to understand action. The hardships of these times have resulted from disorganization. The cause of such disorganization is absurd in its insignificance—the cooperation of hearts has been forgotten. Meeting together in prayer, people forget how to attune themselves for service. Whereas, such a condition is indispensable and is easily attained; for this it is merely necessary that people help one another. To preserve an unusual frame of mind means to proceed to the Fiery World. Under the ordinary conditions of life such a frame of mind is not easy, but precisely it must not be set aside. One should not enter the temple otherwise than prayerfully. In prayer existence is uplifted and made better; therefore each prayer, as also each exaltation, must be better than the preceding one. Each step of the ladder of the spirit must be traversed. How majestic is the Ladder to the Fiery World, which has in a year three hundred sixty six steps by day and three hundred sixty six by night! Every step is distinct from every other, and let each one be better than the preceding one. Joy toward the Teaching, will it not be a true adornment of a step? In each joy for the Teaching is already contained new cognition. Often one cannot express in words this step, given in joy. It is indisputable, and what a veritable mountain is ascended in the prayer of joy! Pains are alleviated by it, the task is made successful by it. No one and nothing can block this joy. Thus shall we have the advantage of success. The same thing may be wished to all, because on the ladder of the spirit there is no crowding. Let each one rejoice at the sheer beauty of a new step. Why should anyone go backward? But it is difficult and burdensome to lose what has been already traversed. Downfall is always harmful, even for the body. One can imagine how ruinous it is for the spirit, for the fiery being. Contact with Fire already produces a special kind of tissue, which glows on the upward, and is reduced to ashes on a downward path. The ladder of ascent is the measure of magnanimity, consequently magnanimity may be achieved daily.

281. Fear of the future is the horror of the World. It breaks in upon life under different concepts. It gradually decomposes the mind and deadens the heart. Such fear is false in its nature. People know that none of their situations are permanent, consequently it is sensible to prepare without delay something for the future. But formless and immobile factors of chaos attach the consciousness to illusory places. One must intensify one's realization of reality in order to recognize the falseness of Maya, and to understand that truth lies only in the future, when we draw near to the Abode of Fire. It is impossible to describe how people try to conceal their fear before the future. They attempt to prove that not the future, but the past must occupy their thinking. They shamefully avoid everything that reminds about the advancement into the future. They forget that this attitude constitutes a dangerous poisoning of space. Even in the purest places waves of such poison can be observed. People also poison each other. But the most health-giving and beautiful thought is about the future. It conforms with the Fiery World.

282. Useful for Hiero-inspiration is the current which is called the Seal of the Hierarch. It can be sensed upon the nape, it shines as a white ray. Through knowledge of Hiero-inspiration it is possible to remember this sensation.

283. A subtle sound is like the language of the Subtle World. It is apprehended without coarse earthly vibrations, just as the music of the spheres is attuned to our subtle vibrations; and thus is received a sensation of the beautiful.

284. Usually people do not understand that a great manifestation is still more sensitive than a small one. Precisely in the great manifestation is a still larger amount of psychic energy required; consequently each obscuration, irritation, or mistrust is especially harmful. When the World is awaiting new conditions it is necessary to manifest special sensitiveness.

285. The Teaching should be read under different conditions, yet the effect will not be always identical. At a time of consternation the Teaching will bring tranquility, at a time of affliction—consolation, at a time of doubt—affirmation, but in order to absorb the reality of the Teaching, one must repress one's casual sensations by penetration into the treasury of Hierarchy. Not merely as a comfort has the Teaching been given, but for advancement upon the ladder of ascent. Indeed, under the special conditions of the world, a deepening of comprehension is especially difficult. Already more than once the world has tottered on the boundary line between mechanics and the spirit. The present is precisely such a time, intensified by the attacks of the dark forces. Multifarious is the bazaar of material rubbish; first of all one must appraise everything in order to set up new values. Thus, the ability to re-appraise within the consciousness will be the threshold of the future. Admission means recognition, and many dark visitors have been admitted by humanity. Such invitations weigh heavily during the transitional state. The heart must be urged to raise its voice for the regeneration of the World.

286. That man is good who creates good. Creation of good is the improvement of the future. One can do good to one's fellow in order to better his existence. It is possible for entire nations to be uplifted by heroic achievement. It is possible to introduce into life most useful discoveries, which must transform the future. Finally, it is possible to improve the thinking of a nation; and in this will be a synthesis of good. How beautiful is thought-creativeness which is not directed toward evil! When the public apprehends all the evil of condemnation, it opens new gates to the future. So much time is thus freed for cognition, for the art of thinking, for the creation of true good; and in these the best fires of the heart are kindled. Such fires are not kindled in evil. Such good will preserve health and to a large extent purify the atmosphere. It is absurd to think that good is an abstraction or a personal merit. It is the salvation of the future, for without it there is no affirmation of ascent. Thus each thought of good is already an arrow of Light. Somewhere it has already exterminated disunity, and any disunity, in malice, is a lapse into chaos. Therefore teach to think about good.

287. We often hear about pains from old wounds. They seem to have healed, the physical tissues have grown together, but pains still continue. Also one may hear that only suggestion can help in these cases. Can it be imagined that the subtle body does not ache when it has been injured? A wound heals physically, but the subtle body may still feel pain. Of course, if the consciousness of a man has been developed, he can by his own command compel the subtle body to become well. But in other cases suggestion is required, acting on the subtle body in conformity with the physical process. Thus do those who know the complex of the organism improve the condition of all its bodies.

288. Current events once again indicate the significance of thought. Already you see that luxury has been challenged. Likewise, you see that magic has received condemnation, and thinking is being directed toward Hiero-inspiration. These two trends are very harmful for the dark ones. Without luxury and without sorcery they are substantially weakened. But they have still left a third possibility—the confusion of weak minds. It is most deplorable that weak minds do not absorb healthy principles. Their instability consumes much energy; therefore We turn our attention to the main issue, in order to concentrate the energy on what is indispensable. You know about Our Banner. Let those carry it who can. Therefore, let us manifest tolerance in all else, and let us compel the dark ones to serve.

289. Blessed is he who instantaneously realizes in his heart the essential reality of Hierarchy. But if the eyes of the heart are closed, then point out to him the order of succession in all that exists. Begin with things of the most everyday life and proceed to the fundamentals of the universe. If then he remains deaf to knowledge, it means he is one of darkness. One should remember that the law of darkness is based on negation. One must not forget that all peoples have had a perception of succession, and in this way they have ascended toward Hierarchy.

290. In truth, Egypt was great in attainments up into the time of Solomon. And Buddha, in a certain sense, received the chalice from Egypt. Thus the foundations of Wisdom have been harmoniously molded. Certainly, the Vedas too had a connecting link with former races. Often Teachings grow in an evolutionary manner, but sometimes due to the depth of Karma the process becomes involutionary. But, withal, there has been an order of succession, and it precisely was a manifest equilibrium of the peoples. Denial of succession is ignorance. The very quality of life, the actual realization of the path, have been founded on successiveness, as an extension into Infinity. Hierarchy itself must be cognized into Infinity. Quite often Hierarchy is represented as being finite, and from this issue all limitations and belittlements. The magnitude of Hierarchy extends into Infinity.

291. It is commendable that the physician has recognized tension in the ears as a fiery manifestation. He should have likewise appraised tension in the eyes and pulsation in the extremities. One may observe many new rhythms manifested as antecedent to fiery energies. But it is imperative that physicians begin to observe certain qualities of illnesses.

292. In primitive religions the fear of God was taught first of all. Thus was suggested a feeling which usually ends in rebellion. Certainly, each one who contacts the Higher World experiences a trembling, but this unavoidable sensation has nothing in common with fear. Fear is cessation of creative energy. Fear is ossification and submission to darkness. Whereas turning to the Higher World must evoke ecstasy and expansion of one's forces for the expression of the beautiful. Such qualities are born not of fear but through love. Therefore higher religion teaches not fear but love. Only by such a path can people become attached to the Higher World. The chains of fear are peculiar to slavery. But the creation of beauty is not slavery, but is reverence with love. Let us compare that done in fear with that done in love. The treasure of the spirit is not from the prison of fear; therefore let us counsel people to love and to be strengthened by the feeling of devotion. No one can defend a place that is fearful to him, but achievement is accomplished in the name of love. Apply this measure to the Gates of the Fiery World.

293. Not without reason did the ancient sages choose to occupy themselves with some art or handicraft. Each one had to acquire some manual skill. They had in mind a means of concentration. Each one, in his striving for perfectionment, thus intensified his will and attention. Even in the few objects which have come down to us, there can be seen a high quality of workmanship. Precisely at present, the time has again come to return to quality in manual work. It is impossible to place spiritual limitations within the confines of machines. It is necessary to take the time to produce a quality of workmanship that will revivify the imagination. Precisely quality and imagination are united on the steps of fiery attainment.

294. It is precisely necessary to understand the sources of antiquity. When their significance is revealed, then will also come new discoveries. There is much to be found, but a savage inclination must not touch the treasures. Let us not reject the logic of evolution.

295. The evil of unbelief inundates the World. Such evil is most ferocious, for it contends with the very essence of existence. It provokes its harborer and in falsehood kills all possibilities.

296. Hiero-inspiration descends through a single basic condition. Neither concentration, nor command of the will, but love for Hierarchy produces direct Communion. We do not know how better or more precisely to express the guiding law than as a flow of love. Therefore it is so opportune to put aside compulsive magic, in order to become imbued with love in one's entire being. As a result, one can easily approach the principle of Existence by a sense of beauty. Precisely, amidst the dissolution of the planet, one must turn to the most health-giving principle. And what can more strongly unify than the mantram—"I love Thee, O Lord!" In such a call it is easy to receive a ray of cognition. Observe this.

297. Often people inquire how to deal with the wills of departed ones. Often such commissions do not coincide with the convictions of the executors. Excepting fratricidal commissions, it may be proposed to carry out everything else. One should not take on another's Karma, the more so since the departed ones continue to develop energy in the direction taken by them. It is truly very difficult to alter a conviction that continues over into the Subtle World. Therefore the fulfillment of testaments is very useful for the harmony of currents.

298. If one would take the trouble to compose a diagram of earthly customs, one could perceive a peculiar picture of the life of the planet. Many customs outlive races and even entire epochs. Even a change of all the conditions of life has no influence upon customs molded by obstinacy. One may be amazed at how old the habits of inertia are, and how they do not depend upon social forms. Therefore I speak so often about the ability to overcome habits. This advice concerns the path to the Fiery World.

299. Hence, everywhere one can perceive three paths: the easy, the difficult, and the terrible. The first is molded through the realization of all successful, useful and good combinations. The second, when certain good combinations are covered by most destructive and harmful structures. Such a path is difficult and is like a race with the eyes blindfolded. The third path, when the ignorance draws one into the darkness of dissolution, is truly terrible. But for this horror people do not have the right to blame others; they themselves have closed their eyes and ears. They have rejected assistance and have admitted chaos into their thinking. Therefore let the Builder follow the first path.

300. Can Light form an alliance with darkness? It would have to extinguish itself in order to become united with the opposite principle. Let a Leader of Light not consider taking into his camp the extinguishers and opponents of Light. Light cannot magnify darkness; likewise darkness cannot enhance the Light, consequently such unions contradict Nature.

301. Information about the language of the Luminaries must be very thoroughly understood. One may have the best combinations and still not apply them. But also one may avoid the most dangerous by heeding signs and directing a zealous striving toward Hierarchy. From this Source it is possible to draw useful wisdom which can lighten karma.

302. Understanding of Light and darkness, as well as of the conformity of the Luminaries with Our Source, is the counsel of the Fiery World. To be pitied is he who hopes to receive Light from darkness. He cannot weigh the treasure in the midst of obscurity. Do not think that such an instruction is an abstract one. On the contrary, each day is filled with associations of Light with darkness. When you bring forward such an ally of the dark ones, no one senses him, only a dog will growl at darkness. One may make a mistake but it is inexcusable not to listen to advice. We do not suppress good-will, but why find oneself in a stormy sea without a life-belt?

303. Let us look at those who come demanding only the new. Take one who so demands but who is even ignorant of harmonization of the centers—can he possibly be given the new? Take one who lacks enthusiasm—can he be given the new? Take one who is ignorant of joy—can he be given the new? Take one not freed from malice—can he be given the new? Take one shaking with envy—can he be given the new? Take one gray with fear—can he be given the new? Take one averse to the Truth—can he be given the new? Take one irascible and moribund in heart—can he be given the new? Many come and ask, "Where then is the new? We are prepared to trample it underfoot. Our thinking is ready to deny it. Our wish is to destroy whatever you say"—such words fill the Earth. The servants of darkness listen for the sake of negation and draw near for the sake of defamation. Discriminate according to negation; it has already found a nesting place in the heart of the servants of darkness. Thus may it often be pointed out, when the cold of negation draws near.

304. The first condition of progress is the non-revealing of the substance of knowledge. One must attune oneself to the essential nature of one's listener, in order not to be mistaken in his intentions. For many ages hence, the fruits of such betrayal may be thus sown, especially since it touches the life of the Fiery

World. People must comprehend the fact that for realization the fluid of acceptance is needed. Repulsion and rejection and revilement are unbefitting the paths of the Fiery World.

305. Many events are filling space. One can see how some of them are rushing there where no possibilities are evident. You already know that human possibilities are distinguished from cosmic possibilities which must be watched. You also know that the nodes of events are like the missile-projectors of the ancients.

306. It may be asked—wherein lies the chief harm of black magic? Over and above personal injury must there also be cosmic damage? Precisely so. The lower conjurations create the utmost harm through the mixture of the elements and the invocation of portions of chaos. One must picture to oneself how in this manner entities of the lower strata obtain access into forbidden spheres and continue to work harm on a broad scale. That is why extensive measures are needed in order to safeguard the planet, which is sick enough as it is. Magic in general must be left alone.

307. Yet it is possible to weaken the harm of black magic to a considerable extent by conscious opposition to it. When one's heart transmits news about an attack, and the dark stars are revealed, one must calmly and fearlessly turn to Hierarchy. Many attacks are stopped immediately. But it would be a mistake to neglect the natural signs of the heart.

308. Wherein is the chief utility of thought-sendings? Besides usefulness for good works, for the sake of which the thought is sent, the principal advantage is in the strengthening of space itself by means of good. Such saturation of space is a great defense of the planet's health. To this end, it is possible to become accustomed to send out good thoughts many times daily, as

spatial arrows. The thoughts may refer to individual persons, or they may be impersonal. The manifestation of good is of great value, and it is not lost in space.

309. Likewise each traveler can fill space with useful ties. Even in antiquity, the dwellers of a community, after a certain amount of time, went separate ways for a while. Such an outspreading fluid network has an enormous salutary significance. One must send not only thoughts but also psychic energy over great distances. The ancients called such a fluid network the fabric of the Mother of the World. Therefore, when the Head of the Community proclaimed the approach of the date of departure, the manifested co-workers rejoiced, for this signified that the net of psychic energy was already strong.

310. Everything of higher significance is found to be in uninterrupted action. A manifestation of attraction is fitting for higher activity. Thus let us fittingly array our hearts in a state of attraction. Nothing else is conformable to great action. One must become accustomed to the understanding of attraction for the Common Welfare; in this will be contained the law of the heart. Likewise all physical laws will be strengthened by attractive actions.

311. In the higher action there will be nothing repulsive; let us leave this quality to the elements of chaos. Let us apprehend that electricity also, which has positive and negative manifestations, will never be repulsive, for the energy is already of a higher dimension. The teaching of exchange and cooperation will not be repulsive. A repulsive thought is already a basis of limitation. A thought of non-admission is contrary to the Fiery World.

312. Even yet invisible, fiery manifestations cast earthly beings into trembling. Currents and rays of the Fiery World agitate even refined beings. Even an unseen manifestation is already unendurable to the heart. How strongly then does it act when transposed into a visible state, approaching the law of incarnate existence! This correlation must be deeply realized. Even some strongest in spirit have fallen into unconsciousness and have turned gray, have become blind and dumb, and have lost the power of movement in the extremities. The manifestation of Fiery Beings ought not destroy our consciousness. In the near future, through their consciousness, people will cultivate their bodies in the receptivity of higher energies. Gradually in this way people can build resistance to fiery epidemics.

313. Once a Teacher was summoned by the king for wise discourse. The Teacher gazed fixedly at the ruler and began to speak about the beauty of his crown, about the brilliance of natural color of the stones, about the lofty symbol contained in the golden circlet, comparing it to a magnet of attraction. To the astonishment of the disciples accompanying him, and to the gratification of the ruler, the conversation was limited to a talk about the significance of the crown. Afterwards the disciples asked the Teacher why he had not spoken to the king about the Universal Principle. The Teacher replied—understanding of the level of consciousness must be the measuring rod. Had I spoken about the Universal Principle, the king would at best have become bored, and at worst would have been cast into the depths of despair. Either one would have been harmful. But it could be observed that to the king his crown was a most precious treasure, therefore it was useful to exalt it and to remind him about the significance of the Crown of the World. Constantly have in mind the best that your listener has. Even if this be a most ordinary object, nevertheless it is necessary to find its utmost significance. Only thus you are made attractive and can open the path for the future. Incompetent and even criminal is the instructor who does not speak according to the consciousness of his listener. Let us remember this parable especially when we attempt to speak of the Fiery World. Any provoked defamation of the Higher Principle molds a heavy karma.

314. Steadfast is he who has devoted himself to the Highest. If there is any wavering in him, it means there has not been a true conception about the Highest. The spirit who is unable to picture to himself the Fiery Grandeur does not know how to ascend to the Highest. Let us repeat that any fear of Fire is already a spiritual blindness.

315. One should know how to correlate many concepts which appear to be different. Thus, to those who do not understand, Hierarchy and self-activity appear as contradictory concepts; whereas Hierarchy requires precisely the development of self-help. He cannot approach Hierarchy who does not understand self-activity. On the steps of ascent, the first condition will be self-help and resourcefulness. One should depend upon the assistance of Hierarchy when all one's self-acting ability has been intensified. Each one knows that according to the extent of acquisition of knowledge the approaches of the Teacher become less frequent, because the man is raised to the step of co-worker. It must be understood that the Principle of self-activity is already a sign of trust. Besides, the trusted co-worker can show reverence for Hierarchy precisely by his complete awareness. Thus, we can assist the Highest Ones through our offerings of self-activity. Failing to understand this Principle, people also have been known to begin to offer blood-sacrifices. But could shed blood possibly be of use to Hierarchy? The exchange of heart energy is a strengthening of cooperation, therefore the manifestation of Hierarchy through self-activity will be the proper ascent to the Fiery World.

316. Truly, one should combine cosmic conditions with our Methods. Thus, when We strongly advocate the abolishment of magic, We wish to help by the natural path.

317. It is well that you understand the development of actions and counter-actions. Actually, with each day actions become broader and involve new strata. Likewise it is well that you understand to what extent the Prince of this World is taking measures for a new battle in all parts of the World. Therefore each manifestation of devotion should be valued. There is too little devotion in the World, each manifestation of it must be encouraged.

318. No doubt someone will ask, "Where are the words about the Fiery World? Teaching about Ethics does not delineate for us the element of Fire." Such people will never understand that the beginning of approach to the Fiery World will be in the assimilation of the fundamentals of life. Only the ignorant will demand the chemical composition of a Fiery Being. But the refined consciousness knows that psychic energy leads to understanding of the Fiery World. Only the heart whispers how it is possible to ascend to the heights upon a polished stone.

319. Even in the most straitened conditions, it is possible to receive restoration and reinforcement. Often a plant is fortified between stones far more soundly than in rich soil. The straitened conditions merely guide the roots into crevices and reinforce them against whirl-winds. The wood-cutter says—why has

a tree taken root in an inaccessible place? Of course, against the wood-cutter.

320. Everyone experiences inner relief when he knows that he is acting as he should. One may explain this feeling as a conscious reflex of the nerve centers, or, as it is said, as conscience, but let us not forget also a cosmic reason for such a state. Right action will be in cooperation with the Fiery World; correlation is the result of it, and the fiery centers of the organism resound with the great thought of space. Thus each right action is not only beneficial for ourselves, but it is also a spatial action. The Fiery World rejoices at right action.

321. That spatial condemnation which takes place as a counteraction to wrong actions was once called "Zephiroth Herim." The people who gave this definition knew profoundly about the bond between Fire and our existence. They understood that besides the law of karma each act touches upon the fiery element. It can interfere with whole spirals of construction and bring on an immediate returning blow. Therefore, the theory of retribution has also, outside of ethical reasons, an absolutely chemical basis.

322. The right path is good for the reason that each of its dimensions is useful. One should not even wonder where the boundary line of the path is. It is possible to become better in any dimension whatsoever.

323. A diver prepares himself for the lowest depth of water. The upper layer of water does not concern him, but he must foresee the entire pressure of the lower layer. So too, in dealing with nations one must have a conception of the lowest consciousness. Everyone who thinks about the Fiery World must be able to understand the thinking of the semi-animal consciousness. One should not ignore the understanding of the very lowest consciousness. On the contrary, one must equip oneself with all resourcefulness, so as to catch the human note even in animal roaring.

Most dangerous it is not to be able to adapt oneself to another's consciousness. How many misfortunes have resulted from words spoken not at the right moment! Manifest resourcefulness.

324. A messenger being overtaken by pursuers throws himself with his horse into the broadest part of the river. The pursuers stop in the hope that the messenger is drowning, but he instead rides out to the opposite shore. The pursuers, in their haste, rush to a narrow place, and drown in the current. Verily, where it is narrow, there it is dangerous. This consideration should be applied everywhere. Seeking the mirage of alleviation does not lead to achievement. The most difficult is the most accessible. People do not wish to understand that persistent quests awaken powerful energies. Therefore let us not strive for the narrow, let us prefer the broad principle.

325. Indeed, solemnity must be cultivated. The ability to direct one's feeling onward and upward will bestow solemnity and a fiery current. We are not far from the Fiery World when a salutary ray can be felt. Perseverance in thinking about the Fiery World already regenerates our nature. Ordinarily we do not feel such regeneration. Only during nodal events do we observe that we have a completely different attitude toward them. At the cleavage of the World we shall sense what we regret and at what we rejoice.

326. In the simplest handiwork, and in music, one can have most instructive experiences. Sometimes one finger alone is not firmly applied at the correct place and thus the full tone is lost; but even then such a misapplication does not at all mean that the fault is irreparable. Some centers harmonize quickly, but others, for many reasons, require far more protracted cooperation. Patience, that great constituent of success, will be tested in such adoptions of the centers. Often, precisely the slower adaptations serve for the good; they not only combine the centers, but, as it were, they unite energy to the future. Thus patience is an adornment of the heart. Each one who is inexperienced in patience will not know how to adapt himself to the Fiery World.

327. It has already been said that blasphemy must be ejected, but one should recognize that each and every blasphemy is inadmissible. Sometimes people are freed from blasphemy only in a narrow circle of concepts, yet their tongues utter grave calumnies in regard to their neighbors. Who can tell what lofty heart channels may be touched by these evil revilements? Therefore blasphemy must be altogether excluded from life as an action unworthy and harmful.

328. A man cannot step forward with both legs at the same time. Such a change of leverage may serve to illustrate the necessity of change of energies. One must become quite accustomed to change of activities of centers. All the centers cannot resound together; in fact, their progress depends upon change of activity. But silence of a center does not signify its death. On the contrary, like a sleeping man it is being renewed in communion with the Higher Worlds.

329. Even in ordinary correspondence conventional expressions are encountered which are understood only by one acquainted with the correspondence. So too in prophecies, we may be surprised by certain expressions not clear to us. But when we recall the time and all the circumstances of the prophecies, we can clearly see that a conventionality of expressions

exists for our time, because the ages have altered many concepts and expressions. One must train oneself in such circumspectness in order not to fall into ignorance.

330. It has been said—the science of luminaries is precise, as the luminaries do exist. But in this let us not forget relativity. Besides the chemism of the rays of the luminary itself, it must be understood to what an extent the atmosphere vibrates at the passage of the heavenly bodies and of waves of cosmic dust. Therefore the astrologer must be also an astrophysicist and an astronomer. In addition, he must perceive the earthly conditions which are working against the rays of the luminaries. Only through observance of these conditions will his deductions be free from errors.

331. Should people be aware of all perils surrounding them? One can imagine the condition of a man who knows how many scorpions or serpents are to be found about him, or how many deadly flies and spiders surround him—a deplorable situation results. It will be particularly dangerous because when a man knows these perils they are brought so much the nearer. Therefore straight-knowledge is best, as it leads by the most secure path and does not weigh one down with a great quantity of needless burdens. Thus, the fiery principle which abides in straight-knowledge is called the wings of salvation.

332. Compare the fire of a smelting furnace with the flame of a raging conflagration; compare harmonious action with the elements of chaos. All salutary rhythms are invoked in order to manifest concordance of action. Therefore schools must develop the rhythm of harmoniousness. We have already reminded more than once about the coordination in gymnastic exercises. Not for war alone, but also for spiritual defense do the crowds need discipline. It is wrong to direct crowds toward bestiality, but rhythm brings harmony into gatherings of people. In this let us not forget the fiery examples. Precisely the fiery principle exists by a special rhythm.

333. One should avoid prejudice both in the great and the small. Many possibilities have been cut short by prejudice. Indeed, the fiery energy is very sensitive to prejudice. But, being aware of this quality of the energy, one can counteract prejudice by means of suggestion.

334. Truly, the disconnection of the chain of Worlds is frightful. No one thinks on a cosmic scale, but one should think about the paths of subtle advancement. One should constantly keep in one's consciousness the fact that thought does not cease moving forward if one's thinking has been carefully guarded. And the union with Hierarchy means that one is not left to advance alone. In reply to the question—are we not abandoned, I answer—Verily, when our hearts are linked to Hierarchy we shall not be abandoned. We can advance in the Subtle World when the Guiding Hand is not rejected.

335. It has been said that humanity must abandon luxury. Not without reason have people themselves so isolated this concept. Luxury is not beauty, not spirituality, not perfectionment, not construction, not benevolence, not compassion; no good concept can replace it. Luxury is destruction of resources and possibilities. Luxury is dissolution, for all structures without rhythm mean only disintegration. One can see clearly enough that worldly luxury has already been shaken, but, as a cure, harmonious cooperation must be found in order to rid the world of the plague of luxury. Egoism will raise the objection that luxury is an earned

abundance. It will also be said that luxury is regal. This will be slander. Luxury has been always a sign of decay and eclipse of the spirit. The chains of luxury are most terrible too for the Subtle World. Needed there are advancement and continuous perfectionment of thought. The encumbrance of luxury will not help one to the next Gates.

336. Good thought is the primary basis of good action. Thought dawns before action, therefore let us calculate the nature of good according to the fires of thought. Faith without works is dead, but such a faith will be a blind reliance, and not thought of good. Thought of darkness also has radiation. Already you know the black spots with red radiation, and how the heat-lightnings of light battle with the dark radiations. Darkness of thought leads to the most monstrous actions. A certain king ordered a sacred Image decorated with horns of diamonds, in order to demonstrate the power of his arbitrary free-will. A certain madman adorned his boots with a sacred Image, and to all appearances nothing happened, for he could not see the ensuing destruction in the Subtle World. He himself was convinced in his madness. It is impossible to measure the Imponderable by earthly standards.

337. When Hiero-inspiration draws one's thought to a definite region or place, it means that circumstances of great cosmic significance are already being molded. Perhaps having such a perception of a place is unexplainable by the earthly state of affairs. Perhaps from the earthly point of view such a country is found to be in a most unattractive state, but the higher law is already determining the place of special tension. Earthly eyes do not yet see, but Hiero-inspiration directs the consciousness thither, where the radiance of Higher Light has been ordained. Thus, above your straight-knowledge shines Hiero-inspiration. Often it appears to contradict the obvious, but it speaks the word of the Fiery World. So too with the sensation spoken about today. Hiero-inspiration directs thither where already the summit is alight.

338. We particularly rejoice when one has recognized the path traversed with Our assistance. This is one of the sensations closest to Hierarchy. Many signs of Our Communion can be discerned. Each such observation will be a strengthening of the bridge into the Fiery World.

339. Each good thought is a powerful lever, for the receiver as well as for the sender. People prefer sendings about earthly objects, but they do not realize that earthly sendings can lead both to Light and to darkness. The effects of earthly sendings depend upon the level of consciousness of the recipient. But spiritual sendings cannot lead into error. They have no path to darkness, but through understanding they can have a favorable influence on earthly circumstances. The Teaching especially pauses on mental sendings. As fiery actions they also have a great significance for the equilibrium of spatial fire. The Teaching must forewarn that disorderly thinking cannot bring benefit for the surroundings. But we must take into consideration that the energy should be useful not only narrowly in one direction, but also for the whole spatial dimension. Let us not forget that Fire, as an omnipresent element, transmits vibrations instantaneously. And no one can arrest the spreading of these subtlest energies. So many times one has to reiterate about cautiousness with energies. Let us not judge as do people who are unwilling to think on a level higher than the earth's crust. When we are striving toward the Fiery World, we must recognize the symptoms of such a condition.

340. With all attentiveness each one must banish from his thinking all that which can bind him to ordinary daily mode of life. Means and opportunities should not be sought in everyday routine. It has been observed to what an extent We do construct in an unusual manner. But right now one must strike still more with unusualness. Look upon this as a means for success. People have entered a narrow place; one should not follow their prejudices. These must be subdued from an unexpected quarter.

341. The wise Leader first listens to his companion in conversation, and only then speaks his opinion. He listens not only to learn the essence of the thought, but also in order to find out what language the speaker uses. The latter condition is of no small importance. It is no great achievement when a law-giver alone understands his own laws. It is necessary that the fundamentals of Existence ring out for everybody, in each one's own understanding. Thus the art of adopting the language of one's companion in conversation pertains to great development of consciousness. It is mastered by Hiero-inspiration or by conscious refinement of attention. No arrogance will be contained in it; on the contrary, it means an interest in the understanding of the companion in conversation. Many a useful consideration is belittled by an odd expression, but the fiery eye discerns these seeds of truth.

342. One can actually observe that many useful things are produced by people not altogether good. There are many reasons for this. First of all Karma; then the assistance of Hierarchy, which makes use of every possibility for the creation of a beneficial situation. Therefore I often indicate seemingly accidental people, and one should not be astonished that such people in themselves are unessential. They can produce that which already centuries ago was prepared for sending.

343. Thought about impossibility definitely derives from the dark principle. Any depression of spirit must be abolished, because this path does not lead to Truth. Men of the most diverse nationalities identically express joy and sorrow. This means that the path to understanding lies open.

344. How then shall the heart endure if it be aware of all the terrors performed? How shall the heart beat when it hears the wailing of a multitude of hearts? Neither the past nor the present will enable it to sustain all the oppressive burden of the World. Only the future in all its fieriness will carry one over to the new shores. Only by casting forward the saving anchor can we make our landing. The farther we cast the anchor the more easily and vigorously do we transfer our consciousness into the Fiery World. For the sake of that World we can improve the consciousness, enlighten the heart, and think about the Good. Nothing else can provide safe conduct for man through all the fields of horror. People do not comprehend the quantity of created misfortunes. The deadening of psychic energy makes people insensitive to reality. Insensitiveness to reality is one of the most frightful epidemics. People turn away from current happenings, and think thus to prolong an existence agreeable to the body. They do not even know how to think about the future. But without the future heroes and regeneration are inconceivable. Therefore, on every occasion let us point to the Fiery World as the goal of existence.

345. No one knows exactly who has died and who has departed. There are many empty tombs and many ashes of wood instead of body. Hence, one should understand the bond with Hierarchy as a manifestation of the Pilot. Even if something is unutterable today, one may understand that the rudder is in Powerful Hands.

346. There are two kinds of people in the world. For some, time is drawn out unendurably long; for others it flies very, very fast. Pay attention to the latter; in them are developed signs of the Subtle and Fiery Worlds. In them are developed possibilities of the labor of eternity. Can one face eternal labor if there remains a sense of weariness of time? Fortunately, already in physical existence it is possible to free oneself from the oppression of time. Not only is constant labor to be considered, but also such a transfer of consciousness into the future that there is no time for cumbersome thoughts.

347. It is beautiful to discern signs of the Subtle World in the midst of earthly life. As a horseman stops on his way to inquire about road signs, so proceeds he who has the future life in his heart. For the earthly sojourn, the only suitable conception is that of the path.

348. He who sows will reap. Nothing can alter the law of Justice. It can be applied in non-earthly measures, but the sowing will have to be lived down according to the strength of consciousness. It is deplorable that even people who know about karma nonetheless continually create a harmful one for themselves. These people, although aware of the Higher Worlds, nevertheless apply earthly measures to everything; to time, to perceptions, and to intentions. Therefore it is often so difficult to lighten karma as much as would otherwise be possible. People seem to resist everything good for them.

349. It has been noted as an astonishing fact that

luck comes through force. This was said in antiquity, and the same expression is heard unaltered today. Only by constant reiteration is it possible to affirm the measures of the Three Worlds.

350. It is inadmissible even indirectly to violate the fundamentals of cooperation. To the concepts of cooperation should be added those of teachership, of guidance, of respect for one's fellowman, respect for oneself, and for those who follow. Precisely at present it is impossible to lessen the significance of cooperation, as a means of broadening the consciousness. One must grow to love cooperation as a pledge of general success.

351. Malice, doubt, unbelief, impatience, laziness, and the other inspirations of darkness separate the earthly world from the Higher Spheres. Instead of following the path of good, people attempt to replace ecstasy of the spirit with various narcotics, which give the illusion of the other world existence. Observe that in many religions there were introduced, as later adjuncts, very clever compounds of narcotics for the purpose of artificially advancing the consciousness beyond the earthly state. Indeed the fallibility of such forcible measures is great; they not only do not bring the Worlds closer, they on the contrary estrange and coarsen the consciousness. Likewise, earthly life is filled with continuous poisonings with which people very affably regale each other. Teachers of all times have taught humanity the pure paths of spirit that lead into communion with the Higher Worlds, but only a few have chosen the path revealed by the heart. A special attention must be given to deliverance from poisonings. A considerable part of the Earth's soil is already infected, as is its surface. Besides narcotics, people have invented many obviously frightful

160

substances which instead of being health-giving bring on spiritual death. Masses of poisonous vapors are choking the cities. People devote much thought to the production of many substances which should be considered far more deadly than narcotics. Narcotics bring harm to the addicts themselves, but deadly gases torment everything that lives. One cannot condemn narcotics enough, but also one cannot sufficiently condemn such murderous inventions. People formerly, at times, fell into error for the sake of illusionary ecstasy, but nowadays they are completely unashamed to kill the intellect and spirit of their near ones, calling this killing an attainment of science.

352. Attention should be paid to each invention of the scientists. They must first of all be responsible for the harmlessness of a new substance. Many metals are being brought into daily use, not only in their pure state but also in combinations. As for that, alloys have attracted human attention from the earliest times. Truly, many useful metals when combined in a certain way produce deadly effects.

Verily, in the future, knowledge will be many-sided!

353. On the subject of narcotics, one may add that since they require a gradual increase of the amount taken, they are as veritable chains of darkness, placing man in a helpless situation. A slave of narcotics, even though he wishes to abandon them, cannot do so without harm to himself. An increase in consumption is deadly, but denying oneself can also be deadly. True, fervent suggestion or autosuggestion can provide a saving outlet. But good suggestion and the darkness of narcosis usually do not dwell under the same roof.

354. People are unable to think about the future usually because they live under the spell of illusions of the past. Imagine a man who many days afterward receives unpleasant news of something which took place previously. This event no longer exists, the man himself has already lived for some time since the occurrence, yet he sinks into the past and loses connection with the future. Surely, the tree of the future must grow, and it should not die from the injury of a plunge into the past. Attention must be paid in schools to the study of the future. Each Leader in his own field will ponder about the future, otherwise he is no Leader.

355. It has already been mentioned that certain peoples used to greet each other by smelling. It may be said—what a dog-like custom! But even in this ugly custom there is a reminder about psychic energy, which was used when people by means of smell, touch, hearing and the eye determined the essential nature of a newcomer. Nowadays there has remained the custom of handshaking, which is also not far from the other strange custom. People have forgotten about magnetism and about spiritual infection. They talk a great deal about hygiene, but they do not consider that contact in itself has significance. Especially at present, during tension of fiery energy, one must think carefully about each created current.

356. To realize that the Teaching transforms the consciousness will already be an essential comprehension, but in order to influence the consciousness one should repeatedly affirm the path of Hierarchy. One must accustom oneself to worthy conduct before the Image of the Hierarch. Thus I say—it is needful to be girded with unceasing prayer. Such prayer is needed now, when the earth is shaken by terrors.

357. Constructiveness, striving for victory, is already a bond with the rhythm of Higher Worlds. Victory is inherent in each seed. The seed in its essence is eternal. It is transposed from one form into another,

but it preserves an ineradicable essence. Guard and honor greatly each grain, each seed of life; in it is contained the highest fiery energy. Even in the finest scientific investigations people will not discover it. It is measurable by fiery measures, and only the fiery heart can sometimes grasp the pulse of the seed of life. But speaking about the impossibility of discovering the seed of life by means of earthly measures, let us not, for all that, distress the scientists; for they still can observe much. The science of the seed can give great benefit. Also one should be reconciled by the fact that the discovery of the seed of life in dense form would lead to the destruction of the World. Correlations of equilibrium would be violated, and no earthly forces could restore them. But when people will apprehend the Subtle World and assimilate the Teaching about the Fiery World, they will advance many steps toward victory over the flesh.

358. Hiero-inspiration must fill all life. This does not mean any breaking away from earthly existence, but Hiero-inspiration should become the sole expression of life. When the Hierarch indicates the approach of a fiery consciousness, then each issued word and thought will conform to the higher solution. It must be observed in life how one's judgment becomes truer and the understanding is unmistakably and correspondingly strengthened.

359. Verily, Hiero-inspiration says—the somnolence of a conqueror is an aspect of most frightful destruction. To resound in rhythm and not to affirm it will be a violation of the law. Victory must bring a harmonious, lawful structure. Victory is not an outburst but construction in all lawfulness. Observe the equilibrium bestowed by true victory. Danger is the friend of victory. If you do not understand it today, you will apprehend it tomorrow. The fiery heart is reinforced by dangers. Thus let us understand the victory of good in all its magnitude.

360. The spiral structure is contained in all currents; one can see the same spiral foundation in all existence. Let us take the example of realization of the Teaching. If one tries to merely read through the Teaching once, there will be no benefit derived therefrom. Only in re-reading is it possible to observe the spiral structure. The Teaching seemingly returns to the same subjects and almost touches them. But the spiral of the current passes upward and brings a new seed of consciousness. The fiery consciousness affirms ineradicable cognition.

361. Certain yogis assume that the secretions of saliva and gastric juice are of purifying value and therefore useful. To a certain extent they are right. During fiery tension the energy of fire stimulates the excretive activity of the glands threefold. In this way, under the pressure of fire which manifests a tripled glandular ejection, a great deal of poisonous matter is carried away. Thus, fiery energy can be useful also during cosmic convulsions.

362. The ignorant assume that the Radiant One comes to avenge Himself upon darkness. But Light does not even kill darkness. More accurately, darkness is confounded and destroyed by approaching the Light. It is very essential to understand that darkness destroys itself when it approaches Light. This the Leader must keep in mind, when the ignorant speak about vengeance.

363. The idea of immediate reward is also to be expected of ignorance. Where, then, are the hours and moments of eternity by which may be measured off portions of the flame? There cannot be any spiritual striving where a demand for reward is obvious. Who can impede the movement of Karma? The flow of Karma must be understood as the approach of requital and of possibilities.

364. Militant darkness is familiar to all peoples under different designations. In the last analysis, darkness remains the most frightful aspect of Avidya. But it is very dangerous when it begins to act. One must courageously meet its attacks in action sustained up to the point of its destruction. It has been said—darkness is as a carpet to the Fiery World. But in order to pass more quickly over the dark terrain, one should become kindled in heart. Thus the Fiery World will be the goal of victory over darkness. If darkness is perilous, then the goal must be great.

365. Notwithstanding all the attainments of science, people grasp with special difficulty the fact that space is completely filled. They talk about microbes, about entities which elude detection, but, for all that, it is almost impossible for them to think about a filled space. They regard it as a fairy-tale if they are reminded that so-called air is filled with creatures of different evolutions. Likewise it is difficult for man to conceive that each breath of his, each thought of his, alters his surroundings. Some elements of the latter are strengthened and draw near, others burn out or are carried away by a vortex of currents. Man is unwilling to understand that he has been endowed with powerful energies. He is truly the King of Nature and the Master of immeasurable legions of entities. It is sometimes possible through powerful microscopes to demonstrate to children in schools the fullness of space. They must become accustomed to the influence of psychic energy. The gaze of an intelligent man reacts upon entities; even under the lens of a microscope small creatures begin to feel uneasy and to sense the currents of the eyes. Is this not an indicator of the living eye, as distinguished from a dead one? On the fiery path one needs to understand the filling of space.

366. A particular confusion has gathered around the problem of offering sacrifices. People at one time arrived at such a state of madness that human sacrifices became customary. But can imagination conceive of a God who would be in need of the shedding of blood? Sacrifices have been mentioned in basic laws, but only later errors and spiritual downfalls have brought mankind to blood offerings. Sacrifice has always been mentioned, but what can be a worthy offering to the Highest Spirit? Verily, only the most purified spiritual striving. Such a basic link serves as the best guarantee of sincere reverence. Such sacrifice is a vital necessity in bringing the best blossom of the heart to the Altar of The Supreme. But people to this day assume that a chip from a small, useless stone can be more precious than the beautiful flower of the heart. Meditation on this question is very useful on the pathways to the Fiery World.

367. Even at the average level, people know much in a rough and disorderly way. It is especially dangerous that people try to perceive not so much an object itself and its significance, as from whom comes a communication and the reason for it. Thus is born the most harmful prejudice. But even wolves can be of use! On a long journey many considerations must be assimilated. Meditation on this is also useful on the pathways to the Fiery World.

368. When I Say—Beware!—it means you must intensify all vigilance of the spirit. It is unwise to strive in only one direction; by this one only limits oneself. The battle requires vigilance in everything. Ancient warriors used to say to the enemy—"If you kill me, so much the worse for you. In Heaven the battleground is more favorable for me and there I shall retaliate." Thus, in their own way did the ancients express the eternity of life and of Karma.

369. "We do not die, but change"—can one speak any more clearly about eternal life? "The wise man proceeds to Me by the Higher Path"—thus conclusively has been ordained the living path. Unjust is the observation that in Scriptures there is no mention of anything about the life of the Fiery World. There are many clear indications, but people evade them. Can it be possible that the element of Fire, continuously alive, can conform to the concept of death, of deadliness? Thus is it useful to meditate on the pathways to the Fiery World.

370. The wayfarer affirms that he goes to the Lord Himself. It is true, people are amazed at such a resolution, but they respect such steadfastness. One must set before oneself the loftiest goal; only then does the road not appear forbidding. One must adjoin the highest quality throughout all existence. One must accept higher measures as alone worthy of the Highest Forces. Only a trained and tempered imagination gives access to the Fiery World. And such meditation is useful on the pathways to the Fiery World.

371. When we touch upon the true path, we sense the power of joy. Our heart rejoices, feeling that our striving is the right one. One can be much grieved, wandering about outside of applicable reflections. But when the consciousness pictures truth, it is filled with joy. Such joy will be wise, for it is based on Hiero-inspiration. And such meditation will be useful on the pathways to the Fiery World.

372. Precisely like an anchor cast forward, the

feeling of Hiero-inspiration leads by the right path. Likewise it is right to think about new people. If tigers are seated on a by-road it is best not to use that road. Verily, the paths are many, but people fear even to think about a new path. Many new people draw near and are growing. Thus, if new people were not in evidence yesterday, it does not mean that tomorrow they will not appear.

373. Amidst the fiery path man mentally strives for acceleration. Many earthly obstacles, attractions and allurements are arranged by the dark forces, yet once he has plunged into Hiero-inspiration and exclaimed—"Let's go faster!", his strength is renewed and, without turning back, he hastens impetuously toward the Fiery World. And such meditation is useful on the pathways to the Fiery World.

374. One may accomplish not a few good actions and then cover them up with one blasphemy. This blasphemy is called the fire-extinguisher; it begets a dark flame and consumes the luminous aura. Repeat to friends that the boundary line between disparagement and blasphemy is a very fine line. Disparagement of one's neighbor must be eradicated from daily life; this error surely opens the way to the blasphemy of the Highest. He who understands containment will also understand the cosmic harm of disparagement.

375. The Fiery World is as filled as the other spheres. Likewise, beings of different evolutions, yet of the fiery degrees, come together for cooperation. While those in the carnate state, under the influence of chaos, almost entirely fail to understand cooperation, and while in the Subtle World group cooperation is found, the Fiery World is distinguished by full cooperation. And such meditation is useful on the pathways to the Fiery World.

376. Out of useful meditation is molded complete attainment. First of all, one will become definitely ashamed for all chaotic thinking. It will become impossible to counteract anything good, no matter in what form it be expressed. A difference in expression only is a subtle one, and we must regard it as a cobweb in the light. It is a joy when it is possible to refine one's thoughts.

377. Deliberate outward ascetic practices are nothing but vanity and self-worship. Recall that a Saint revered by you could not be distinguished outwardly by the eye of the newcomers. Thus He demonstrated that the external appearance is not the fiery body. And such meditation is useful on the path to the Fiery World.

378. The explanation of a number of manifestations connected with magic methods reveals that the will was expended to no purpose. We have a long list of those who disturb the elements without promoting in the least the Common Welfare. Some of them replace artificial methods with good thoughts, but many prove to be only irritators of the elements. Yet, such overstepping of the laws not only works harm to man himself but disturbs the harmony of space to great distances. Even a plain bowman in the forest cannot guarantee that none will be hurt by his arrow. And such meditation is useful on the path to the Fiery World.

379. Once Akbar, in the midst of the State Council, ordered that the Book of Laws be brought to him. On the book appeared a small scorpion. The meeting was interrupted and all the councilors gazed at the small, poisonous insect until the servants killed it. Akbar remarked, "The very smallest miscreant can suspend judgment pertaining to the state laws." Thus also on the path to the Fiery World the most insignificant detail can do harm. Only the heart can determine the fine point of balance between striving and caution. If the minds of all of a group of statesmen became dumb at the sight of an insignificant scorpion, then a cobra could throw an army into retreat. A warrior can be intimidated by a mouse if in his heart burns not the fire of faith and striving.

380. Actually, it is more difficult to arrest a thought than to generate it. For trial, first the conception of thought takes place, then its strengthening and concentration, and only afterward is it possible to test oneself upon deliverance from thought; the latter is not easy even physiologically. Thought creates a special fiery substance. Its crystallization, then, means that dissolution is required, and this process demands new fiery energy. So-called intrusive thoughts are often the result of a fiery flash which cannot be balanced by further treatment. The thought has succeeded in being crystallized, but the extra fiery energy needed is not there. Therefore deliverance from a thought is recognized as an extremely needed indicator of the proper conversion of fiery energy. A great deal of suspicion, a great deal of envy, a great deal of revenge can be stopped through liberation from intrusive thoughts. So, too, in space, intrusive thoughts cause actual calamities. It is all right if these thoughts are directed toward an unselfish deed, but if they be about injury or destruction, the digging of such a channel in space will be unworthy. Often intrusive thoughts are not expressed aloud in definite words, and therefore influence by suggestion is made difficult. Learning to free oneself from a thought can be of great assistance in advancing toward the Fiery World.

381. Inability to free oneself from intrusive thoughts can produce no small difficulties in relationship to the

Subtle World. Let us imagine that certain hazy, perhaps even unpleasant, condensations from the Subtle World have been manifested; their forms have struck the imagination and produced thought about them. Precisely the substance of such thought will attract still more strongly these entities and assist their condensation. Naturally, thought is nutritive. Precisely in this manner are formed the so-called ghosts. Intrusive thoughts give them density, and people cannot free themselves from them, because primarily they do not know how to free themselves from their own thoughts.

382. Mastery of thought is a fiery action. The concentration of thought and its projection is a fiery action. But a far greater fiery energy is demanded for liberation from a thought. We have read about great saints who scorned earthly luxury and freed themselves of earthly accumulations; but, first of all, they had to conquer their own thoughts. Through long tests they learned to summon thought and to dismiss it. When We speak about mobility, it is necessary to have in mind primarily mobility of thought; and such meditation is useful on the path to the Fiery World.

383. The man who does not think about the Highest is turned into a creeping reptile. Proceeding in body, proceeding in thoughts, proceeding in spirit, advances the consciousness toward the Fiery World. One must acquire this knowledge of locomotion in order to obtain indefatigability and unquenchability for ascent. Even in the middle stratum of the Subtle World, the dwellers do not know how to strive upward. They have not been accustomed to thinking about such aspiration. They are obliged to learn to reconstruct their consciousness, but this is not easy and could have been attained much earlier. Thus We

advise to meditate about a quality which is useful on the path to the Fiery World.

384. Warnings are useful in all cases. Earthly ailments ought to be anticipated. It is impossible to provide people with a panacea if the conditions of life are not purified. People dream about deliverance from cancer, that spiritual scorpion, but they do nothing to preclude its germination. You already know that the remedy given to you is one of the best against cancer, but it is also necessary to make use of vegetarian diet, and not to indulge in irritating smoking and drinking. Furthermore, one must expel imperil, and then the indicated remedy will be a good shield. But people usually do not wish to renounce all the destructive excesses, and they wait until the scorpion stings them. Likewise do other terrible diseases spread, as the dark gates are held open for them.

385. During transmission of thought at a distance a very indicative manifestation is observed. Thought is sent in one language and received in another. Does not this prove that psychic energy acts not verbally, by means of cerebral processes, but precisely by the fiery energy of the heart? Furthermore, it must be observed that not only is thought given utterance in another tongue, but also the expressions issuing from the consciousness are found to be the most customary ones. Such a difference of words may often impede recognition of thought transmission on the part of inexperienced observers. But notice that the passage of thoughts acts in accordance with the meaning, not the words.

386. Nausea and excretion are recognized by Yogis as a self-defense against poisoning, which can be not only from food but also from hostile currents.

Undoubtedly such currents can impinge on man and react like physical sensations.

387. Often accidental shocks restore sight, hearing, and other lost senses. Does not this force one to think the crystal of imperil and other sediments have been suddenly expelled from the organism? Thus, strive to understand why sometimes in antiquity shock was applied in treatment of certain illnesses and paralysis.

388. Relativity of names is understood only after a deep study of the subject. Sometimes a spatial process is called, as it were, by a personal name. But human action is comparable to fiery energy. Actually the two processes are quite indistinguishable in their essential nature. This is why ignorant deniers often charge the Teachings with over-stressing sacred things, while at the same time they fill their own speech with superfluous and conventional abbreviations and coined words.

389. Spiritual laziness is a very common retarding condition. One may encounter people quite capable spiritually, and yet at the same time, going absolutely backward from sheer laziness. Each one can see how the best possibilities are carried away in a whirlwind simply because of laziness of thinking. Such meditation is useful on the path to the Fiery World.

390. Many times have We pointed to the loss of equilibrium in the conditions of Earth. If people do not pay attention to these alternations of increasingly unprecedented cold and heat, then very likely they will soon be obliged to experience fiery uprisings.

391. When people pass through a room filled with electric power lines they are usually very cautious. But who will sense all the currents of space, infinitely more powerful than a fraction of enslaved energy? When the fiery heart says—today the currents are heavy, or light—such perception should be regarded with careful attention. Such feeling is perfectly real, as real as the treatment by currents at great distances. Only one who has experienced the reaction to currents at a distance apprehends their reality. But too many people ignore these sensations, primarily through laziness of spirit. And such meditation is useful on the path to the Fiery World.

392. A certain prior of a monastery, when sending the monks on a journey, always exhorted them with the words—"again is our cloister expanding." He knew that there can be no spiritual estrangement, and that such affirmations of the journey only augmented the dimensions of the cloister. Thus ponder when some of the brethren begin a new march.

393. Drops of Grace fall into the chalice of heart's joy. Could there be a greater joy than that during the fulfillment of a Mission of the Brotherhood? Thus must it be understood for those who go forth or remain guarding the Ashram. Very important is the vigor which grows out of the Power of Grace.

394. Only a blind man does not see the hastening of events. You have read about a rare conjunction of the Luminaries. Yet still more significant is the chemism produced by such an infrequent manifestation. Nations can alter the quality of their thinking, yet they pay no attention to rare manifestations, not even to phenomena.

395. Karma is action—it cannot be defined otherwise. Some think it possible to define Karma as effect, but this would make it like a retaliation, and thus would belittle the law. He who walks by the right path will arrive at his goal. Each deviation will lead away from the direct path, and people will begin to talk about a heavy Karma.

Verily, when a traveler wanders into a thicket he is

obliged to surmount many obstacles in continuing his original action. Karma is the product of action and is itself action. And such meditation is useful on the path to the Fiery World.

396. Sleep affords communion with the Higher Spheres. Sleep proves that without such communion people are unable to exist. The explanation of sleep as bodily repose is a most primitive one. Without sleep people can usually go on but a very short time before their thinking falls into a most ailing state; hallucinations and torpor, and other signs of an unnatural existence appear. The organism strives for the life-giving exchange, and does not find the ordained way. As We said, sleep can be brief on the heights, where the currents of communion can be especially nourishing. People may remember about meetings in the higher Spheres or in the lower. The dense body can impede such essential communions, but sleep as such will be the gift of the eternal life. And such meditation will help on the path to the Fiery World.

397. The conjunction of the Moon, Venus and Saturn is indeed rare. Precisely such a conjunction produces a chemism of extraordinary force, and it may be remembered that We pointed out the assistance of the Luminaries in actions useful for the world.

398. People who aspire above the Subtle World toward the Fiery World are right. We continually mention the Subtle World, but with all means We direct to the Fiery World. A man who is prepared in his meditation for the Fiery World is even in the Subtle World uplifted to the Higher Spheres. We are all uplifted or we descend, and if our thought has been allied with the Fiery World there results a great magnetic attraction. And if our thought is confluent with Hierarchy, the bridge of great daring becomes real.

399. If the fiery heart feels that somewhere harm is being inflicted, it is not in error. No matter that the injurer first of all harms himself. Enough has been said about Karma. One must observe how personal injury is transformed into spatial evil.

400. Eternal Fire fills all bodies, and through them is unified with the higher fiery energy. In such a manner is the Universal sap worked over and over. This mysterious, ever self-regenerating substance cannot be named otherwise. Thus everything manifested serves for the renewing of the Eternal Substance. The circle serves as the best representation of the cooperation of energies.

401. A certain tranquility is required for sleep. The necessity for this transitory state proves to what an extent our organism needs a special striving to effect a change of conditions.

402. You have noticed that at times We do not repeat certain names. This circumstance depends upon varying causes and currents. Even a paper kite is not flown every day.

403. Some people walk into the future with full trust. Whence can be drawn such invincible confidence? First of all, from communion with Hierarchy. But understanding of the Luminaries also strengthens the consciousness. Moreover, there is still a third circumstance which has no small significance. Actually the three Worlds exist in full cooperation. The affirmation of many earthly beginnings takes place in the Higher Worlds. You know about earthly teraphim; there can be likewise teraphim of the Subtle and of the Fiery World. Not infrequently entire structures, prior to their earthly realization, have been created in the Higher Worlds. One may read in the ancient Scriptures about Heavenly Cities; in fact, they are being constructed in reality upon different spheres, and thus a magnetic attraction is created. Often people do not suspect that their teraphim already exist in various forms. At times the clairvoyants perceive such actual images, and erroneously carry over what they see to the earthly plane, whereas the earthly reflection is formed later. But one fact is unquestionable—precisely, the existence of such teraphim—it strengthens the consciousness of man. Can it not be that certain cities already do exist, and named people live in them? One may walk into the future as assuredly as if the delineations of the city were before the earthly eyesight.

404. Verily, special caution is needed, in spirit as well as in earthly circumstances. One must deport oneself as if a conflagration were imminent. In the hands is affirmation of the future. Each caution will be valued as an action of wisdom. I have Spoken.

405. Precisely each economy is needed, both in things and in spirit. You cannot take into account all the directions of the currents. Everything is indeed temporary, but the spirit is tempered in the midst of vortices.

406. Cooperation based on personal feelings is not steadfast. Besides respect for the labor itself, reverence for Hierarchy is indispensable. Under the whirl of personal feelings people will bob about like cork manikins, and will jostle each other and be occupied with spasmodic actions. But each labor, in its very nature, does not tolerate convulsions. Labor is a fiery action, but the fire must not lead to convulsions. Moreover, external personal feelings can impede recognition of new possibilities. How many beautiful actions have suffered due to transitory personal mirages! And such meditation is useful on the path to the Fiery World.

407. One should break away from personal

expressions as from harmful habits. A feeling which has been tempered in the fire of Hierarchy will not become distorted. Thus learn how to balance feelings on the truest scales. Much patience is needed in order to be able, without losing the feeling and the heart, to check upon their quality on the scale of Hierarchy.

408. One should not return again to a meat diet, if the organism has already become accustomed to a vegetable one. There can be exceptions only on account of hunger; but usually a handful of maize or rice can be found. People often do not suspect how meat can constrict and disfigure the aura. But a disturbance may be felt particularly when the organism has become accustomed to the advantages of a vegetable diet. People sometimes discriminate less than animals in the matter of food and its quality. Such meditation is useful on the path to the Fiery World.

409. Good for him, who, by experience in life, and reverence for Hierarchy, has freed himself from the sense of personal property. Verily, he has shortened his path. But if the coarse, carnate garment does not permit as yet the liberation of the consciousness, then one should not be violently deprived of property. Such compulsion only provokes stubbornness and malice. Only by personal example and inculcation of the Teaching is it possible to attract people to the quickest true understanding of Life.

Traveler, do you understand what a beautiful attainment awaits you, when you approach, winged, the Fiery Abode, and nothing is scorched by the Eternal Flame?

410. Listen, but judge not. Often precisely an outflow of poison liberates a man for a new path. The Teaching extends aid not by negation but by attraction.

411. The path of equilibrium is attained through

meditation. One should often repeat to people that reading, or even understanding, is not meditation. One must become accustomed to meditation. Cognition from without must furnish the impulse for the fiery process of meditation. Fire is the great equilibrator. Absolutely consciously must one approach the Path of Balance, where there will be no more waverings and doubts—where there will be only Great Service.

412. One should not guess at one's place in the Fiery Hierarchy. We are all hard workers in the Sphere of Light. Earthly measures cannot express the dimensions along the path to the Fiery World. Each one has a fiery particle, but how and where it is transfigured is not a matter for earthly conjecture. Yet we distinctly sense when something accomplished by us is worthy of the Fiery World. Thus each one must be in tune with this sacred feeling. In this he will be a true co-worker.

413. There is a manifestation of new tensions. The enemies invent new tricks; but let us be as a rock and we shall arrive at victory. One may rejoice that each attack brings new friends. Such friends are inconspicuous, but they can be likened to the cement of a building.

414. An infected man does not sense his infection for a long time. Since this is true of physical disease, the more readily understandable is such a process of incubation in diseases of the spirit. One may be amazed at the fact that physicians do not attempt to observe the origin of a malady of the spirit; hence, it is more difficult for them to observe all the fiery processes. But if physicians deny such fundamental conditions, then whither may people be directed in order to learn the causes of their unprecedented sensation? Likewise, scholars and school-teachers are of no assistance—thus people are left without advice about the

most important inceptions of disturbances of body and spirit.

415. Curative assistance at a distance must invoke a strengthening of the blood-circulation and an increase in the manifestation of tension. One should realize that sendings require special fiery energy, but at the conclusion of such a sending the excessive tension tells upon the entire organism. Healing is an action of great selflessness.

416. Powerful artificial lightnings can purify the lower strata of the atmosphere. The tension must not be too great, for matter should not be decomposed. It must be purified, not dissolved, because disintegration would be equal to the admission of chaos with all its consequences.

417. The ancient prophecies say: "When all becomes darkened, then people fancy that everything is permitted them." Actually darkness makes people insane. Daring is not madness. Everyone who dares is conscious of ordained possibilities, but the madman manifests opposition to the law of Existence. There is a fine boundary line between madness and daring. The torch of the heart is needed in order to find this boundary. Having once entered the domain of madness, one can hardly turn back again to a wise daring. Rishi were daring; saints were daring; but they did not admit madness, for it is first of all hideous. It leads to obsession, with all its dark consequences. How ugly is the picture of the obsessing entity trying to expel from the body the subtle vehicle! There can be nothing more hideous than the spectacle of two subtle bodies disputing about one earthly envelope.

418. Achievement and testing have a deep scientific significance. The fiery element requires pressure; it scintillates during tension, and therefore labor is a fiery action. Indeed, achievement, as the crown of labor, is the most radiant tension of fire. Let us apprehend labor in all its significance, as both mental and physical. Knowing how to respect the degree of each labor indicates a containment which is suitable for the Fiery World.

419. Why do people only sometimes sense physically the presence of subtle beings? They are surrounded by them, yet they rarely sense them. Here we touch upon a very remarkable fact. Earthly beings feel it when the subtle dwellers contact their consciousness, either because of their own desires or because of affinity of auras. Then people experience that trembling which for the ignorant turns into terror but which for those who know signifies the stimulation of the fiery element. Not many, since childhood, can consciously recognize this tremor, which has even been called sacred.

420. Sleep-visions acquire significance as soon as the connection with the Higher Worlds is realized. In fact, when a man has grasped the meaning of sleep as sojourn into the Subtle World, he knows that by means of this condition he can recall very important and lofty communions. Each book about the Subtle and Fiery Worlds should not omit mentioning associations through sleep-visions.

421. The Yogi can sense heat and cold independent of external causes. Such transcendental perception relates to the Subtle World. It is sufficient for a dweller of the Subtle World to think about warmth or cold or other sensations, and the energy of thought will invoke them immediately. Thus, thought constitutes a laboratory for all reactions. Therefore, on the path to the Fiery World We insist so much on watchfulness over thoughts.

422. In vain do people complain about being separated from the Subtle World. Many see the subtle dwellers. Many grasp the speech of that plane. Many sense aromas not of this earth. Countless manifestations can be named, both among people and among animals. Only obstinate prejudice prevents people from understanding reality. So many people have been saved by indications from the Subtle World. So many matters of state have been decided according to information from Beyond. Not only do ancient epochs furnish examples of this, but the most recent past can provide indisputable facts of such continuous relationships. The Earth cannot be isolated from all the Worlds. Even the material senses, contrary to all ignorant superstition, transmit feelings of the Subtle World. When the consciousness has been refined, then can be expected precious contacts which will be perfectly natural.

423. Striking phenomena can be observed around spilled blood. Animals not only sense the blood but fall into agitation and terror. It can be noticed that even dried blood produces the same symptoms as fresh blood. Precisely the fiery emanations of blood are unusually strong. Not by accident did the most savage sacrifices require blood, as a means of excitement into intoxication. Likewise the black mass needs blood as a strong stimulation. For such purposes animals are used. The resulting sharpening of scent for the invisible is very strong, the more so because blood attracts many lower entities.

424. The Lights of the Mother of the World resemble the pillars of the Aurora Borealis. Very rare is the phenomenon when the microcosm—man—can be compared to the Macrocosm. Ur. has seen such a manifestation. It responds to the pressure of world energy.

425. Sometimes people reach such a height of absurdity that in their every thought about the future life they consider it the end of earthly existence. At the same time they do not hesitate to arrange their earthly affairs many years in advance. Such actions merely indicate how obscure is the thought about the future life. Consequently, all Teachings, all manifestations, all scientific attainments do not reach the consciousness.

People will demand from you new remedies, new indications about food—merely for bodily comfort, but not for the improvement of their own future, which is in need of constant and solicitous construction. People are unwilling to imagine that their earthly life is shorter than the very briefest stop of a railway train. The worthy wayfarer, in a short night's lodging, is concerned not with troubling his host, for his consciousness is directed toward the goal of his journey. But travelers of the Great Path often think only about the night's lodging, unconcernedly forgetting about their destination. Petty thinking is not commensurate with the Great Path! Therefore the fiery path will be the path of consciousness of the future. Every traveler who is enlightened by thought about the eternal path can proceed in joy. In each such march one must carry a particle of eternal Fire. One should approach the Fiery World with a whole purpose, with all desire, with the whole heart.

426. We repeat about the Fiery World. Should one contend with it or grow to love it? Can one struggle with that which fills all that exists? Will not such a conflict be a most senseless action? Will not love for the Fiery World provide a most powerful magnet? If in the earthly existence love is the most creative principle, the stronger it is in the Higher Worlds.

427. The path of joyous achievement is a

hundredfold shorter than the path of mournful duties. How steadfastly must this ordainment be kept in mind by the travelers of the fiery march! Only the sign of achievement raises them above danger, but the significance of achievement must be cultivated in the heart as joy of the spirit. One cannot discover the best path if one's eye does not follow the star of achievement. Even the obscurities themselves must be illumined by the one Light. Nothing, no one, is ever forced to turn back into darkness.

428. Day-dreaming must be transformed into disciplined thinking. The ancient sages advised mothers to pass on to their children tales about heroes, and to acquaint them with the best songs about great deeds. Is it possible that humanity nowadays wishes to renounce this wise advice? The Fiery World is first of all open to heroes—to those who achieve.

429. People condemn the Teaching for the fact that it does not condemn a fellow-man. One may imagine how many new listeners could be acquired by censure of a neighbor! Such an impediment will be the darkest veil on the path of advancement.

430. There are people ignorant to such an extent that they would say to the entire formula of life—is that all? Yet, they themselves do not carry out a single piece of advice. No explanation is of assistance where the heart is silent or has become ossified. It is fearful when people require as help only the tricks of legerdemain. The consciousness of such people is worse than that of a savage. Nothing pure and guiding will penetrate through the crust of chaos. People are unwilling to contemplate the extent to which they surround themselves with a destructive aura.

431. Manifestation of their will leads people to different attainments. Whoever has accustomed himself to thinking about a pit of trash invariably will find it. Beautiful is the law that thought guides man. Beautiful thought does not lead the way to darkness.

432. Written meditations about the Teaching are useful. It may be proposed to co-workers that they accustom themselves to such work. They can select portions of the Teaching near to them, and compare them with other Teachings. In this way there can be observed the imprint of the times upon the very same truths. The task of investigating this evolution will in itself be a much needed labor. We are opposed to condemnation, but the comparison will be, as it were, the polishing of the stone. Through love for the subject one can find new comparisons and beautiful points of contact. Such meditations are as flowers in a meadow.

433. New life can begin from each instant. There can be no obsolete life, save perhaps in our conception of it. Yet, for what do we exercise and regenerate our thinking? Precisely for a new life. Let us not understand this as a personal concept, as egoism. Such a life of selfishness would be cringing. But no one who crawls can ascend. A new life in the name of Good is built up in cooperation. Such a life kindles many fires. Let us not forget that thought of good kindles in its path a great number of lives. The poisoning of space with evil thinking is no new thing. But selflessness of the heart directs thinking to the kindling of new torches. Surely, wise is the law which invokes good thought for the lighting of new fires. The manifestation of the new, eternal sparks of the Fiery World will be actually new life.

434. "The Heavenly Forces are now invisibly serving with us"—a new conception of the reality of Invisible Space is already a step toward the actuality. We cannot pride ourselves on our cognition so long as the

Invisible World does not grow in our consciousness. Thus, let us be on guard against everything which sways our thought away from that of good for others. The revelation of fiery thought will be accessible to benevolent thinking.

435. One of the brilliant fiery actions will be the taking upon oneself of the pain of one's dear ones. The fiery heart burns like a beacon and takes upon itself the infirmities of the surroundings. It will not suffer from such a treatment if the quality of the aura of the ailing one does not send dark arrows to the savior. Even a strong fiery heart can be wearied by such an unmerited response. The more so since it is not easy to consume another's pain in the fire of one's heart. It is particularly difficult when such pains arise from unworthy actions. And such meditation is useful on the path to the Fiery World.

436. Let us turn back to the conditions which facilitate the taking of medicines. It has already been observed that in the past certain peoples took medicine with singing as an aid, others with lamentations or incantations. Aside from the meaning itself of the words of the incantation, it is highly essential to observe the rhythm, which was altered depending upon the ailment. Present-day physicians should study these means of better assimilation of medicines. Not only suggestion but the quality of rhythm can produce an important result. Let us neglect nothing of the ancient heritage.

437. One of the most visually beautiful fiery actions will be the convergence and divergence of auras. This beauty can be likened to that of the Northern Lights, and in it is expressed a multitude of psychological moments. One may observe how carefully the radiations draw near, how the protective network palpitates and flashes, as a preliminary to resounding harmoniously or to becoming darkened. The full and complete life, its chemism and magnetism, is concealed in the space around a man. We await the time when people will begin patiently to photograph auras. Then it will be possible to observe the movement of light on a cinema screen, when the film will reflect the sequence of movements of the aura. You know that for successful photographing many subtle conditions are required. Often even a physically uncomfortable room can yield good results. You have excellent prints of subtle beings, photographed under ordinary conditions. Also, you know that when you decided to improve the physical conditions the photographing failed. The chief factor of success lies in internal, invisible circumstances. One must apply great patience, and exclude any irritation or wavering. Any fiery chaos merely darkens the film. Also, there will be no especially clear visions when there is a confused frame of mind. But when the necessary harmony is reached the photographing will be easy. Many external conditions can have an influence; therefore it is better not to bring in new objects once the needed vibration has been established. Any disorderly exclamations are also harmful. The principal element is patience.

438. Amid fiery actions there must be observed not only striking phenomena but also many transitory, hardly perceptible manifestations. We must often pay the utmost attention to the latter. The character of man is formed not so much by phenomena as by constant fiery waves. If people await only phenomena, and neglect the hardly perceptible sensations, they will occasionally be shaken, but they will not acquire a fiery continuity of consciousness. The Teaching must not burden the nerve centers with shocks. On the contrary, the ascent will be steadfast when people realize within themselves the existence of benevolent vibrations. Let people grow to love the very thought of the Fiery World. Let such counsels be a daily matter. One cannot attract to oneself the power of this element without love and the heart impulse.

439. The entrance of human manifested fire is not accomplished without realization of responsibility. In such realization will be contained that refined solicitude and carefulness which conforms with knowledge. Blasphemy, direct and indirect, is impossible in the refined consciousness. No falsehood conforms to the fire of truth. Amid actions and cares one should not be distracted from thought about Hierarchy and about the Fiery World, great and nearby.

440. One may observe that during an earthquake the throat becomes quite parched. In this manifestation is seen the tension of fire. Thus, a great number of concepts are diffused into life, one has but to notice them.

441. Each Teacher must possess the quality of listening. This is necessary for the treatment of many ailments. It is necessary to promote the outflow of all harmful substances. The Teacher sees when the dying fire is liberated from the covering of gray ashes. A healthy fire leaves no ashes behind. It completely transforms that which passes into the eternal. So, too, must thought be purified by fire. Each day man must reflect about something eternal. Such meditation will be useful on the path to the Fiery World.

442. Someone says that he wishes to attain cosmic consciousness; let him better think about purifying his heart. Let him not so much imagine himself as conqueror of the Cosmos, but rather let him wish to cleanse his consciousness from dust. One cannot penetrate beyond the limits of the law without wishing to become transformed in the approach. Verily, the baker of bread, in both the spiritual and material sense, must not think only as to how to get his own fill.

443. The experienced physician advises the convalescent not to think about his past illness, and urges him to think about the future and about favorable circumstances. Thus, any reminder about the past illness is cast out, not only physically but spiritually. One should apply the same simple method in all the situations of life. Particularly during fiery actions, when fire is palpitating because of darkness, one should not think about darkness and its reaction on fire. A manifestation referring to the future will kindle the heart. The most oppressive thing can be dispelled only because of the future. Fools clamor about finite life. Can eternal life possibly be terminated? So many terrible things have to be performed in order to violate life! Even wild beasts do not dare to return to the dust of the abyss.

444. Boldness should be combined with caution. Otherwise boldness will be madness and caution will turn into cowardice. People who can picture to themselves the entire complexity of fiery waves can appreciate the advice of caution. The Yogi does not forget full caution; in it there is respect for the great element and reverence for the Fiery World. One may understand that it is necessary to exert the utmost caution, as when passing between rows of the finest vessels. If these works of fiery labor require such carefulness, the fiery waves themselves enlarge the path of our observation of the heart.

445. Among psychic maladies the most frightful, almost incurable, are treachery and blasphemy. Once a traitor, always a traitor. Only the strongest fiery shock can purify such an infected brain. If such a criminal condition emanates from obsession, this is likewise not comforting. Is it possible to conceive of cooperation with a traitor or a blasphemer? They are like a plague in the house. They are like a fetid corpse. Thus, the Fiery World has no consolation for traitors and blasphemers.

446. It can be observed that the Subtle World is approaching the earthly. Even fiery sendings do not miss the Earth, but the consciousness of people can sometimes be far from the reception of these manifestations. The word is uttered, but the consciousness is silent. There is not even a restlessness fitting before great events. The death-like state of the consciousness is staggering! One can understand how gradually the subsequent Teaching must be given! A readiness to apply the Teaching to life is noticeable only in rare cases, but the fiery manifestations tarry not. Not having been transmuted by the human consciousness, they flow into dangerous channels.

We would wish that that which is taking place could keep people from madness. Planets are speaking with bloody rays, but this ancient science is also dead in the hands of destroyers. Worthy minds suffer under the waves of madness and ignorance. Light-mindedness is not in conformity with the discoveries of science. Indeed, each one may prepare an abyss for himself, if he wishes. But madmen have no right to drag worthy ones along with them. In addition, very grave is the last conjunction of the luminaries. It is necessary to contact carefully the fiery forces.

447. The embryo of the spirit actually does not begin with human evolution; its manifestation refers to an indescribable fiery process. That is why you apply to man the words—kindling of the spirit. Precisely, given to man was the kindling of fire, which dwells in all the manifestations of creativeness. One should remember that powerful energies have been entrusted to man; therefore, whoever does not kindle the spirit does not fulfill his destiny. Precisely, self-perfection itself is first of all attained in the consciousness of the manifestation of spirituality. There can be no approach to the Fiery World without the manifestation of spirituality. This must be remembered by all.

Some suppose that spirituality consists in the reading of spiritual books. There are many such readers but few who carry out.

448. Assist all who strive for perfectionment. Discern where there is striving and where possibility of defection. Discern where there is love for ascent and where the restlessness of doubt. He is a false teacher who elevates doubt into dogma; distrust is not the aim of the discipline of the spirit kindled by Truth.

449. One should observe that during especially grave conjunctions of the constellations strong spirits appear. One may investigate in history how systematically powerful helpers are sent from the Fiery World who take upon themselves the burdens of the World, and who plant magnets for the future. One must study the history of the planet from all angles, in various branches of knowledge. One should recognize the winding paths of humanity as a science connected with the basic laws of the Universe. The study of the chemism of the luminaries should be introduced without delay. Already much valuable material has been accumulated which once again confirms the bond between all the Worlds.

450. What We mean by caution must be definitely understood. The ignorant may assume that caution is inaction or the gloom of fear. On the contrary, caution is a strengthening of action, watchfulness and courage. Caution is very necessary when fiery waves are provoked. One can resist such tensions by means of the magnet of Hierarchy. When I indicate caution, it is necessary to direct the heart, aflame, to Hierarchy.

451. People may be surprised that a place especially full of the danger of earthquake remains without the influence of fire. Let them ponder about this.

452. Will it be superstition if a man observes all that takes place around him? May he not be justified when gradually he learns to appraise all that is invisibly occurring? If all digits are fluctuating and there is no constant magnitude, then how attentively should one refer to the multiformity of manifestations of the Cosmos! Precisely this incalculable diversity helps the individual experiences of the spirit. What seems impossible today is apprehended tomorrow, thanks to a new chemism of the luminaries. India has just experienced an unprecedented upheaval. It may be expected that the earth will not quickly settle down in certain places. Amid the shocks there occurred several visions of the Subtle World. The disturbance of the atmosphere created waves useful for the manifestation of subtle bodies. Though these manifestations be of brief duration, still such observation is useful. Likewise, one can observe amidst the most ordinary conditions special vibrations and resoundings. One should distinguish all such subtle manifestations.

453. One may rejoice at each new step of life. A new combination of elements produces a fiery refinement. Never do the dark forces experience the joy of union with Hierarchy. One person considers each hour as the last, but another is conscious of each hour as a new one and foremost. Such attitude is the fiery one.

454. Many legal statutes have been invented by

humanity, but the most immutable has not been pronounced—that of cosmic right. It is easily seen how often this law is applied and how it guides life. One may often observe how something impossible according to human laws is nevertheless accomplished. The worthlessness of all human precautions is often astonishingly evident. One cannot but feel that something over and above earthly reasonings guides circumstances; in this something are the will, cosmic chemism, and the most immutable magnet. Cosmic law brings destined people close to world problems. Sometimes they cannot explain how unexpected details are put together. But they realize that their heart is aflame. Thus it is, as it were, joined to something unalterable. In conformity with this immutable law it is possible to pass over the most dangerous abyss. Such full authority may be called Hierarchic, but when we add to this the chemism of the luminaries and the delineations of the far-off Worlds, it is then possible to define such a right as cosmic.

455. When we sense the Cosmic Lotus, we must go forward in full consciousness of the mission. We must precisely understand how the fire of our microcosm resounds with the great fire of the Macrocosm. Can the obligation of Service in Fire possibly be a small one?

456. It may be observed how the organisms of people respond to the tension of nature, how fiery people must sometimes emit blood, in order to proportionately free themselves from the tension. It may be remembered that upon ancient images there can often be seen the Intercessors for humanity. Such an achievement of selflessness is not fiction. The path of the Fiery World runs through the adamants of selflessness.

457. Divide everything into four shares: the

first—for the Highest; second—for the Common Weal; third—for your fellow-man; and fourth—for yourself. But the hour comes when only three parts remain, for the fourth will be swallowed up by the second. Such divisions are called fiery. Nothing but the heart can indicate the boundary lines between them. But let the sequence be flamingly inscribed.

458. There are good tears and ugly tears—thus did ancient Egypt discriminate. The first are from rapture, from love, from achievement; the second are from anguish, from malice, from envy. Not long ago a scientist turned his attention to the difference, depending upon the impulse, in the composition of tears. Indeed, secretions differ widely in nature when contrasting feelings introduce harmful or good ingredients. But tears, being a very pure manifestation, can yield especially useful observations. Of course such observations require time and patience.

459. You have seen dark spatial spots. Likewise you know the turbid formations resulting, as it seems, from spatial combustion. Also, you know the radiant spatial formations. Everything becomes alive and is flamingly transformed, likewise do one's senses vibrate. The experienced observer knows that his eyesight sometimes grows dim and then again clears up. The same thing happens with the hearing, the sense of smell, touch and taste. Thus can be observed complete mobility of all our functions. In fact such fiery nerve-responsiveness to the Macrocosm represents a refined condition, but only a few take into consideration such a conformity with the external world. Imperfection of consciousness obstructs all observations.

460. A most ancient expression—to look through fire—has been subjected to incorrect interpretation. People have understood it in the physical sense. They began to make use of a wall of fire in order to develop clairvoyance. But for natural ascent such artificial methods are not only unnecessary but even obstructive. Indeed, one should look upon earthly things through the fire of the heart; only such inspection can foil the snares of Maya. But fiery tension requires time and patience and devotion. I cite this example as demonstrating to what an extent the ancient wisdom has been distorted, being expressed in the gross forms of magic.

461. It is right that you do not forget the significance of soda. Not without reason has it been called the ash of Divine Fire. It belongs to those widely given remedies which have been sent for the usage of all humanity. One should remember about soda not only in sickness but also in health. As a bond with fiery actions, it serves as a shield against the darkness of destruction. But one should accustom the body to it gradually. Each day it should be taken with water or milk, and in taking it one should, as it were, direct it into the nerve centers. Thus can one gradually acquire immunity.

462. It may be observed that I Advise you to concentrate mentally on certain individuals, but it should not be thought that the effect can reach only these persons. Lightnings act upon a certain extent of space; so, too, do the lightnings of thought fly through a great expanse and touch upon many circumstances. The central person will be the focal point, but no less useful is the influence on the surrounding area. A thought of welfare is as a nursery of good.

463. So let us expel any feeling of prosperity, and let us evoke all vigilance, realizing how unfitting is the thought of comfort in Infinity, and let us adopt vigilance as an eternal prayer. Thinking about the Fiery

World, one should be especially conscious of these concepts. Thus, let each writing about the Fiery World end with advice about unceasing watchfulness.

464. People are so carelessly engulfed in an everyday routine of life, that even the most striking thing appears dull to them. Ingratitude, laziness, unwillingness to respond with the heart, all are engendered by darkness of existence. But the fiery path shines with the fire of the heart.

465. You think correctly about gratitude. The best expression of gratitude will lie in the realization of the greatness of the Mission. The Service is so great that each step already constitutes an achievement. Each day, with each thought, something significant is done. A great manifestation gives rise to innermost solemnity. In this solemnity there is also expressed gratitude. Solemnity is one of the best magnets. Hence, let us think about the greatest, for by this measure all else can be covered.

466. In studying the fiery paths, one should remember that history greatly distorts the facts. Of course, to a certain degree one could reconstruct them, but such an impartial attitude practically does not exist. When there are inquiries about certain historic figures it is often impossible to reply, as all the conditions surrounding them have been misconstrued. Likewise, it is impossible to indicate certain medicinal and scientific methods, for they were surrounded by most unusual circumstances. Therefore, there is much that requires preparation of consciousness, and this is slowly accomplished. This is why We so stress becoming accustomed to patience and carefulness.

467. Actually, Fire cannot remain in a state of immobility. When We speak about the spiral of ascent, We have in mind a fiery structure. The movement cannot be arrested, for this would be incompatible with spatial Fire. People attribute many properties to Fire, but the principal condition remains unobserved. Fiery Guidance is the basis of the resplendent element. It must be remembered that flame is directed upward, it cannot turn its arrow downward. So, too, the adherents of the Fiery World cannot go downward. If We observe a fall downward it means that Fire of the heart is drooping. Let there stand before you examples of radiant Fires! One can choose a beautiful affirmation through such Torches from the Earth to the Fiery World. Let us not droop, for this is unbecoming to Fire. Let us not belittle any fiery significance, nor tokens, which you have seen and felt. Let us assist friends to proceed flamingly, for non-affirmation of the Higher World is self-destruction. And let us consider the Fiery World as the most proximate, the most guiding, the most flaming. It is necessary to think about the Fiery World as our destiny.

468. The expenditure of psychic force takes place voluntarily and involuntarily. Lofty spirits continue the sowing of good unceasingly. In this it must not be forgotten that the refined consciousness cannot avoid a certain weariness. Such fatigue is very diversely expressed, but usually it falls on the physical organs, which are far more subject to illness. Therefore We counsel a wise caution. It is difficult to stop the flow of psychic forces, but it is always useful to protect one's physical forces. One should not interrupt the current of Good, but each caution will be but a strengthening of this beneficent stream. The fiery path especially must be guarded by a wise circumspectness. We have already considered many fiery qualities, but no fewer still remain. Only the unwise will look into the succeeding book without assimilating the preceding ones.

469. The Silvery Lotus of the fiery heart is not often manifested, even to lofty spirits. But separate petals of the fiery Lotus can be seen, and in accordance with them let us assemble the entire flower. But if this fiery wonder is even once evoked, and viewed by the heart, then from that hour the heart's path leads upward, toward eternal attainment. Let the ascent be of extreme steepness—We prepare a hand-rope for those who have resolved to ascend.

470. Rejoicing is a pledge of joy. We know how precious is each particle of joy, in it is a step of victory—*Vijaya*!

Let the path be victorious!

Traveler, gather together all reflections about the approach to the Fiery World.

Traveler, realize that there can be no other path.

Traveler, you must be conscious of the Fiery World as something real, and which nourishes life.

Traveler, apprehend that your earthly life is the very smallest part of your existence.

Traveler, accept the Guiding Hand.

Traveler, fear not to look upon the Gates of Light.

Meditations taught you to purify your consciousness. Thoughts sent to you make you a co-worker of fiery attainments.

Thus approach the third part of the path to the Fiery World.

AGNI YOGA SERIES

Agni Yoga Society
www.agniyoga.org

Printed in the USA
CPSIA information can be obtained
at www.ICGtesting.com
CBHW071123010424
6198CB00028B/472